LGBTQ+ REVOLUTION 2.0

LGBTQ+ REVOLUTION 2.0

JILL FREDENBURG

NEW DEGREE PRESS
COPYRIGHT © 2020 JILL FREDENBURG
All rights reserved.

LGBTQ+ REVOLUTION 2.0

ISBN   978-1-64137-944-1 *Paperback*
        978-1-64137-752-2 *Kindle Ebook*
        978-1-64137-753-9 *Ebook*

CONTENTS

INTRODUCTION 7
AUTHOR'S NOTE 15

A VERY BRIEF LGBTQ+ HISTORY: MOMENTS IN THE HISTORY OF THE GAY RIGHTS MOVEMENT IN THE UNITED STATES THAT INFORM OUR PATHS FORWARD 27

MISTY: CALLED ME OUT 55
VISHAAL: OPPORTUNITY AND MEDIA REPRESENTATION 61
ROBYN: VULNERABILITY TO ACTIVISM 73
STACY: Q AND OC 85
RIVER: ASEXUAL IDENTITY 93
XANY: COMING OUT IS ALMOST ALWAYS SCARY 103
ARI: ONLINE COMMUNITY 111
ALEXIS: GIFTING BOUNDARIES 121
TRISHA: IT CAN BE SMALL 129
VALERIE: FINDING VOCABULARY 135
HAFSA: IDENTITY IN MULTITUDES 145
FANFIC AS DISCOVERY 153
CASSANDRA: FINDING COMMUNITY IN SUBTLETY 159
KASH: COMING OUT TWICE 167

ALAYNA:	WHY STIR THE POT?	179
KIM:	YOUR IDENTITY IS YOURS	189
BLAIR:	EXPLORATION	197
ALEX:	WHAT WOULD YOUR LIFE LOOK LIKE WITHOUT SHAME?	203
SHAPE OF LOVE		211
SEEK OUT EXPERTS: IN KNOWLEDGE, SUPPORT, AND LOVING KINDNESS		217
	ACKNOWLEDGMENTS	227
	RESOURCE LIST	231
	APPENDIX	235

INTRODUCTION

In a beat-up, black, regular-ole car parked in the empty lot of a college campus, with the smell of a moneyed, freshly mowed lawn in the air. That's where Cassandra* (she/her) realized her sexuality would be something she'd constantly have to redefine as important. For the remainder of her life, she'd need to re-prioritize her sexuality as a true aspect of her identity, re-assert again and again as a valid, worthy part of herself both *to herself* and *to those around her*.

In late 2012, Cassandra had begun dating a new guy. He was the nerdy type, quiet and smart. This fresh relationship came with all the regular questions: When would she ask about his favorite music, childhood hobbies, and values? Religion?

Dietary habits? Weird fears? Aspirations? All these inquiries filled her mind, adding weight to each of her late-night conversations with him.

Among these inquiries was the topic of sexuality, something most straight folks don't need to discuss. But how would she go about bringing this up? How would she come out to her new boyfriend? At the time, Cassandra identified as **bisexual** (attraction to two or more genders).[1] She still uses this word often but is also comfortable with **pansexual** (capable of being attracted to any gender), and she felt her sexuality needed to be made known in order for their relationship to be honest and strong.[2] Biromanticism and panromanticism are sometimes included within these labels, though some people are sexually attracted to certain groups or to no one, and romantically attracted to other groups or no one. But would he react poorly? Would he try to sexualize this part of her identity for his own gain?

To wrap her head around how she would discuss this aspect of her identity with her new guy, Cassandra found herself on a late-night drive with a friend she'd known since they were baby-faced sophomores in high school. Eric's* black car had been a frequent Taco Bell-tinged clubhouse for their small group of friends. Escaping Thursday evening family awkwardness in favor of a laughter-fueled night driving around East Memphis had become a ritual, one to rely on for hipster tunes and cuddle fests. There were few physical and emotional boundaries, and this

---

1 Ashley Mardell, *The ABC's of LGBT+*. (Mango Media Inc, 2016.), 8.
2 Mardell, *The ABC's of LGBT+*, 8.

made everyone feel accepted, celebrated, and whole in their moments together.

Tonight, though, it was just Cassandra and Eric. Whenever this particular duo found themselves parked together under the cool blanket of a Southern evening, they spent the time solving each other's problems. Nineteen-year-olds do, after all, make the best therapists.

The two disagreed frequently, but the act of listening to each other and providing time for real feedback was special and crucial to both of them; their personal growth was impacted by these check-ins. So naturally, when Cassandra proposed these questions surrounding her new love interest to Eric, she expected the same attentive, thorough responses she'd grown used to. And he did provide this comfort at first, assuring her that she need not be nervous to ask questions of her new beau, until she brought it up—the "bi" thing.

"I mean, do you *have* to tell him?" he asked.

To Cassandra, the car suddenly felt very different—like the doors were more restrictive than she'd noticed before, closing in around the pair.

She did not know how to respond. The fact that she was attracted to women was important to her. This personal importance made the conversation imperative. This element of her being wasn't going to vanish just because her new partner was a man.

I could sense the confusion she'd felt at the time, as she told her story over the phone years later. The hurt that came from her friend's lack of support was still evident in her voice.

> "My bisexuality doesn't disappear because I'm dating a man. That just isn't how sexuality, or at least *my* sexuality, works. But it was frustrating because it made me feel like I was making a big deal out of something unimportant."

Of course Eric's response was frustrating! Often bisexuality and pansexuality get written off as phases or kinks or are ignored altogether, when in reality these identities are pretty common. According to a UCLA study from 2011, those who reported any same-sex sexual behavior and any same-sex sexual attraction at all are substantially higher than estimates of those who self-identify as lesbian (women attracted to women), gay (men attracted to men, though this is often used as an umbrella term for all of the LGBTQ+ community), or bisexual.[3] The study revealed that 19 million Americans (8.2 percent) report that they have engaged in same-sex sexual behavior, and nearly 25.6 million Americans (11 percent) acknowledge at least some same-sex sexual attraction.[4] The discrepancy between the rates for self-identifying as lesbian, gay, or bisexual and the rates for admitting same-sex

---

3   Gary J. Gates, "How Many People are Lesbian, Gay, Bisexual, and Transgender?" (Williams Institute), April, 2011.
4   Ibid.

encounters or attraction makes those who are questioning their sexuality feel abnormal and often prevents those who "own" their questioning from having a more fluid sexuality being taken seriously by others.

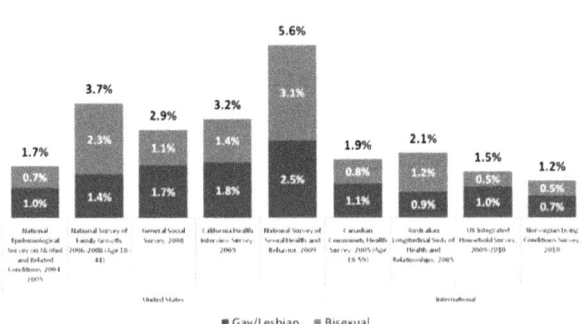

Figure 1. Percent of adults who identify as lesbian, gay, or bisexual.

The Williams Institute

Cassandra's story and these statistics really resonated with me. The first time I tried to broach the subject of my bi/pansexuality with my family—the only time I unsuccessfully tested the waters (literally, in some sense; we were at my family's annual beach trip to the Outer Banks in North Carolina), I received a similarly irritating response.

My uncle had brought up my dating life since I had been single for a while. As I was about the age of fifteen or so, the appropriateness of this topic for conversation was questionable, though I think many adults have a hard time connecting with their teenaged family members and assume the awkwardness and humor that comes with speaking about romantic flounders is a safe bet. My uncle was wrong in this case, because I had been considering and scrutinizing my own sexuality for at least two years leading up to that point, making the conversation ripe for a particular kind of discomfort for which none of us were ready.

His simple, "So, what's your type?" turned into discomforting jokes when I admitted, naïvely trusting him, that I didn't really have a type; in fact, I didn't think I was limited by the genders of prospective partners.

"Trish, did you hear that? Jill is bi!" my uncle yelled across the kitschy family beach blanket.

I don't remember my mom's response. I think there was an awkward laugh and a silence between everyone before I interrupted, quickly saying, "I mean, I'm just figuring it out."

I wasn't expecting to be capital O-U-T with my family on that trip. Yet, somehow, even that horrible announcement didn't out me fully, because it wasn't taken seriously. My uncle did not know the right thing to do, obviously, or else he would have simply said, "Oh, that's interesting," to make me feel safe in that moment, rather than announce our conversation. But this was his reaction to discomfort.

I am now ten years older, wiser, and although I am sure of my identity as a pansexual woman, this memory is still gut-wrenching. His comments initiated a learning and relearning journey for me, exploring the world's interpretations of my sexuality. What has helped me establish my positive mentality toward my sexuality and romantic preferences throughout my life have been the communities I've built for myself and the knowledge that I am not the only person struggling with external pressures to conform to hetero-centric ideas of sexuality and love.

---

*Starred names are fictional, used for privacy

AUTHOR'S NOTE

So much has happened in the LGBTQ+ community over the past twenty years, and because of this, there's often a sense of "We've made it." Sometimes this book will use "**queer**," an umbrella term taken on by some in the LGBTQ+ community, though not everyone is comfortable using it because it has historically been used as an anti-gay slur.[5] On June 25, 2015, the US Supreme Court struck down all state bans on same-sex

---

5   Ashley Mardell, *The ABC's of LGBT+*, (Mango Media Inc, 2016.), 13.

marriage, marking a monumental step for the gay rights movement.[6] From the founding of the Society for Human Rights, the first documented gay rights organization in 1924, to the first National March on Washington for Lesbian and Gay Rights in 1979, to Billy Porter becoming the first openly gay black man to win the Emmy for best lead actor in a drama series, the LGBTQ+ community has had many wins.[7]

But for people like Cassandra and me—bisexual women who have to re-validate ourselves to others—there still seems to be so much work to do in order to feel included in this powerful community.

I started writing this book with the hope that the process would help me understand how experiences like Cassandra's and my own fit into the larger movement surrounding LGBTQ+ identity. What I have discovered has made me excited for the next wave of LGBTQ+ rights. I've seen broader, more intentional conversations around inclusive policy and social practices that promote safety, vocabulary, and community-building.

This wave is ushering in a new future for the LGBTQ+ community, a future where trans- and gender-affirming pronoun-usage isn't seen as an inconvenience, and bisexual people do not need to produce a list of same-gender partners to prove their queerness.

---

6 Adam Liptak. "Supreme Court Ruling Makes Same-Sex Marriage a Right Nationwide," June 29, 2015.
7 "Stonewall Inn: Through the Years," *American Experience*, PBS, accessed May 1, 2020.

I, personally, like to think of myself as part of this LGBTQ+ Revolution 2.0 and hope you see yourself as part of this positive learning path too.

Like many of the people you will read about in this book, I am someone who cycles between labeling myself as bisexual, pansexual, and queer depending on my audience, and I have gained much of my early LGBTQ+ education from YouTube. I have become an ever-learning ally to the trans, asexual (ace), gay, lesbian, and + communities with which I do not expressly identify. I am in a position of both great privilege and great curiosity. I look forward to the advances the LGBTQ+ rights movement will achieve next in terms of gender acceptance, racial equity, and disability rights, among other areas.

I benefit from the work of Marsha P. Johnson and Mark Segal; of Kathy Kozachenko and Susan Sontag. I benefit from the work of hundreds of unnamed queer individuals and allies. I am hugely lucky, for now is arguably the best time in our nation's history to be an LGBTQ+ person. I am also acutely aware of the current tensions within and around the LGBTQ+ community and know that we can all do better for ourselves and our community.

In August of 2017, after completing my undergraduate degree (Art Major, with minors in International Relations, Netflix binging, and caffeine, thank you very much), I traveled to Narva, Estonia, on a Fulbright scholarship to teach English and Media Literacy to groups of young people there.

Narva is a small city, located in Ida-Viru county. This city is at the extreme eastern point of Estonia, separated from Russia only by the Narva River. While Narva holds the title of the country's third largest city in Estonia, it only has a population of about 57,000 people.[8] Like any LGBTQ+ person living in what most Americans would consider a small town, I was quite concerned about my queer identity becoming *too* apparent. In hindsight, this concern was somewhat silly, as the heteronormative assumptions there were even stronger than those I had grown up with in Tennessee. (I'd likely need to paint rainbows on my face for anyone in Narva to question my sexuality.)

However, LGBTQ+ people often seem to magically find other people like ourselves. We attract each other somehow.

In Estonia, I worked for an amazing organization as my primary service location. This youth-empowerment program was never explicitly LGBTQ+ friendly as far as I could tell, but the program had some support from the Estonian government (as part of the European Union) and provided a space where Narva's youth were able to reflect upon and explore their interests and goals.[9]

During the nine months I spent in Narva, a small group of students, individually from one another, came out to me as LGBTQ+. I'm still not sure why they felt comfortable

---

8   "(Narva Linn, Ida-Viru, Estonia)—Population Statistics, Charts, Map, Location, Weather and Web Information." City Population. Accessed May 1, 2020.
9   "FRA—European Union Agency for Fundamental Rights," Fundamental Rights Agency. September 7, 2012.

approaching me with this information. Some said they had sought out my Instagram and Facebook accounts and seen the subtle rainbow emoji on both. Because of that rainbow, or potentially due to some general queer vibe I may give off, or maybe simply because I was a twenty-something woman from America, they got the feeling I would be a safe person with whom to share their sexual and gender identities.

I didn't think to ask why they confided in me, not even after the fourth student asked to see me after class and asked if I had any online resources they could use to learn more about LGBTQ+ identities. I was too stunned with the students' confidence in their own terminologies, the assumptions they'd made that I was a good resource, and their direct questions. I gave them all the support I could and shared links to the age-appropriate resources I'd used when I was younger. I still don't know if my efforts were sufficient, but I like to think that talking with someone helped them feel seen, at least in some small way.

I briefly mentioned to a supervisor that I was having interesting conversations with young people about identity, specifically about nationality and sexuality. She encouraged me to respond exactly as I had been responding, which was reassuring.

Looking back, I wish I had asked what marked me as a safe person in which to confide. However, I was so focused on balancing my personal safety with the responsibilities of the role I was fulfilling through the United States Department of State's funding that I prioritized getting the students as much information as I could without "crossing a line." I basically added a bunch of incredible LGBTQ+ people to their Instagram feeds for them, wrote down the Trevor Project's links, and googled about Russia's historic homophobia to help me understand the environment in which their identities were evolving. Given the systemic Russian homophobia and nearly 90 percent ethnically Russian population in Narva, safety for LGBTQ+ students was a concern. While Russian individuals are, of course, not inherently homophobic, my students told me about plenty of anti-queer biases they saw in school systems, religious discussions, media, and more.

I realize now (two and a half years later, at the time of this book's publication) that I could have done so much more for those Estonian students. At the time, however, I had severe "Imposter Syndrome." Doomed to constantly revisit my internalized bi-phobia, I did not believe I had the right, as a **cisgender** (gender identity matches the one assigned at birth) woman who had happily been in a relationship with a cisgender man for years prior to my Fulbright, to be an information source for young queer kids in Estonia.[10]

Had I been serving students in the United States, I'd have suggested they speak to a counselor and keep my email address on file for any specific community-building or empowerment questions. In America, I knew how to make space for myself, to a point. In Estonia, I didn't feel "gay enough" to be a valid resource for young folks who were realizing they might be LGBTQ+. I wasn't sure how to proceed. I was nervous.

---

10 Ashley Mardell, *The ABC's of LGBT+*, (Mango Media Inc, 2016.), 8.

My time in Estonia was difficult and thrilling, harsh at points, but full of wonder and new experiences. I came home with a queer zealousness I hadn't felt before. I wanted to encourage American LGBTQ+ people to cherish resources more fully and be even more vocal about welcoming young people, especially those still figuring themselves out, into the community.

Shortly after I returned from Estonia, I got engaged to my incredible partner. This engagement, so soon after my return, shook up the way I viewed my LGBTQ+ identity. I wasn't going to be a queer girl with a boyfriend trying to understand how to empower queer youth anymore but a woman taking part in the sexism and homophobia-riddled institution of marriage.

Amidst all the excitement around being madly in love and thrilled that my partner wanted to be with me for life, I also felt as though I was signing up to be "straight-presenting" forever—a privilege in America and in many other societies because public displays of love were never scary for us due to our gender presentations. He was wary of public displays of affection in unfamiliar spaces because ours is an interracial relationship, a burden I did not know he held until more recently. But our romantic lives weren't pried into with bedroom-questions and skepticism or judgement in the same way LGBTQ+ couples' relationships are often scrutinized.

I had found a soulmate—a person I am convinced I was meant to love and who fills me with a kind of strength and drive I had not known was possible before meeting him. The magical balance of work and luck that has benefited our relationship is something I quietly wish for all of my close friends and family to find in their partnerships, so I said yes and am so glad I did.

Even with that joy, though, I was terrified that queer spaces wouldn't welcome me because of my husband and that the somewhat quiet sexual and romantic identity I'd held since I was sixteen was going to become a dormant part of my life, a fun fact to pull out when my kids were coming of age but not something to feel proud of. And that thought made me feel physically ill for months.

I went from happily only being out to my close friends and boyfriend to vocalizing my identity more during the 2016 presidential election, subtly supporting people by confirming my identity in Estonia, and feeling like I'd be muddying queer spaces if I entered them. That was so much to handle in such a short time, and I did face some questions.

When I entered graduate school, I promised myself I'd prioritize finding the LGBTQ+ resource center on campus and surround myself with other queer people—people with whom I felt I would likely feel more myself. In this quest, I took any small opportunity that presented itself to meet other people from the LGBTQ+ community.

One of the first activities I participated in early in my first semester was a focus group geared toward LGBTQ+ people—one centering around dating apps. I had very little experience with dating apps and websites, as my partner and I got together when we were both eighteen, around the time Tinder and Bumble were making their way to Tennessee. But I decided to go to the focus group meeting anyway because

I figured my brief stint on OKCupid—one of the first times I'd ever selected "Bisexual" as an identifier for myself on a website—would be worth discussing.

When I entered the classroom, I was impressed that there were ten people present in the meeting, which, for a program of sixty people, wasn't bad. As we all went around to announce our names, pronouns, and sexual orientations for the sake of the focus group research, I was the only person to use the term "bisexual." A couple of people used "queer" and the majority of the group identified as "gay" or "lesbian."

I remember thinking that, likely due to my nervousness to be around a new group of people, I was blinking too much—the room was hot and dry in DC's August warm front, and my contacts felt as though they were scratching at my eyeballs. I so desperately wanted to be included—a reflection of an insecurity that came from years of constantly presenting disparate versions of myself to different groups of people— so I was probably a bit overenthusiastic during the focus group meeting.

Afterward, I learned that when someone in the meeting heard I was engaged to a man (my now husband), she scoffed about it and visibly rolled her eyes, bringing the topic up later on with a small group of people without my knowledge.

Her behavior hurt in two ways. First, she was outing me to people I didn't know. While I am out and was planning to be open about my sexuality in graduate school, I wanted to control who knew and when, at least as much as I could. To someone outside of the community, the issue of controlling who knows about one's sexual identity may seem small, but being queer was my information to give, not hers. Her lesbian identity did not absolve her of this inconsiderate behavior.

Second, she was discounting my identity, taking it less seriously, because of the gender of the person with whom I fell in love. This episode wasn't the first time I felt excluded because I wasn't "gay enough" for someone, but she tossed me through a similar loop that my uncle had that day on the beach.

This experience only pushed me to be more vocal, to surround myself with supportive people who make time to really *hear* me. With the encouragement of a few of these folks, I started this project, and I am so glad that I did.

Conversations around both bi and pansexuality are not necessarily more or less difficult than others, but the heteronormative assumptions that plague all of us are a different style of challenge for people who often date the assumed heteronormative gender. When Cassandra casually told Jaquelin, her oldest friend, that she was interested in another woman, Jaquelin was offended that Cassandra hadn't explicitly told her about her sexuality. Though Cassandra had been constantly posting bisexual content on Tumblr, a site on which Jaquelin was equally active, this accidental conversation turned into a huge deal. But Cassandra had simply been operating, for years, under the assumption that Jaquelin had read her online posts and had known Cassandra's sexual identity.

When telling me this story, Cassandra joked,

"I just think it's funny that in my brain I was out to her. But it took me talking about kissing a girl for her to even question my 'straightness.' Because we all still assume you're straight until proven otherwise."

In this book, you will hear from non-gender-binary folks who still have to convince their gay and lesbian cisgender elders to use their proper pronouns. You'll cringe at the hilarity that is queer Tumblr fan-fiction and find power in individual exploration and identity-layering. You'll see examples of awesome LGBTQ+ representation in the media and find narratives from people who are *still figuring it all out*.

As with many identities in this book, please be mindful that one person speaking about an identity is not the definitive statement about this experience. The people in these pages were generous enough to share their experiences with me, and I am thrilled to be able to share their stories with you. Everyone's experience of sexuality and gender is different; even two people who share the same label (e.g., identify as bisexual) may experience bisexuality differently. The reason for LGBTQ+ Revolution 2.0 is to prioritize the conversation—the open doors—over assumptions and hard lines. Different experiences within identities are also prevalent due to other factors like one's racial identity, socioeconomic status, disability status, and spiritual upbringing. All of these various contexts can have a huge impact on the specific ways any person experiences gender and sexuality.

This book is for people both within and outside the LGBTQ+ community, people who are questioning, and people who want to learn to be better allies. Most of all, this book is for those of us who live and identify outside the lines, who don't fit in any particular box, but who are still an important part of the LGBTQ+ community and who want to help each other thrive.

We, as LGBTQ+ people, sit under a gorgeous, living rainbow umbrella, one that has shifting colors and titles and fabrics but is resilient and waterproof and impressive both close up and from a distance. We have come so far in the past few years, and every day we continue to march toward a brighter and more inclusive future. I am so excited to have you with me on this journey as I explore the LGBTQ+ Revolution 2.0. While we all may be at different points on the spectrum of gender, presentation, and sexuality, the most beautiful part about our community is that we are ultimately all in this together. So, let's listen to one another.

A VERY BRIEF LGBTQ+ HISTORY:

MOMENTS IN THE HISTORY OF THE GAY RIGHTS MOVEMENT IN THE UNITED STATES THAT INFORM OUR PATHS FORWARD

BEFORE STONEWALL

We cannot have a bright, shiny, upgraded version of a movement without recognizing that the original is still living, breathing, and hugely deserving acknowledgment and celebration. LGBTQ+ Revolution 2.0 is not a negative statement about the rich histories and narratives that have brought us to this point, but a second wave—similar in many respects to the second wave of feminism—expanding upon the important conversations that draw from the previous movements.

What is often labeled as an umbrella term, the "gay rights movement" in the United States has evolved quite a bit in just the last few decades. Even the reclamation of words like "queer" and "dyke" have been and still are contentious within the LGBTQ+ community because these terms were used as slurs.[11] Reclamation has entered the conversation because so many laws prohibiting "same-sex" activity have been struck down fairly recently. Many people born after 1990 may not have grown up aware of these laws, but we benefit from the activism of those who tore these barriers down. Though changes in governmental leadership in the United States can make these issues worrisome, lesbian, gay, and bisexual individuals have been allowed to serve openly in the military since 2011.[12] Couples of any gender makeup can now legally get married and adopt children in all fifty states.[13] But, as many inclusive, progressive gay rights proponents know, these wins have not been seamless and have received enough pushback to potentially face retraction. Transgender individuals, for example, were allowed to serve openly in the military from 2016 until March 2018. A new ban was put in place at that time, harming the troops already serving and those who wished to serve in the near future.[14]

---

11   Alexander Cheves, "21 Words the Queer Community Has Reclaimed (and Some We Haven't)." Advocate. Accessed June 4, 2020.
12   "Military Service Members' Rights," Justia.gov, accessed June 4, 2020.
13   "Same-Sex Couples Can Now Adopt Children In All 50 States," Governing.com, accessed June 4, 2020.
14   Helene Cooper, and Thomas Gibbons-Neff, "Trump Approves New Limits On Transgender Troops In The Military," *New York Times*, March 24, 2018.

These barriers mandate an LGBTQ+ Revolution 2.0. LGBTQ+ folks and allies must celebrate our accomplishments and find joy in small movements, but we must not be content in half-finished laws and social norms. Those of us with additional privileges in socioeconomic status, for example, are equipped and in stable environments to push for the rights of the LGBTQ+ umbrella, and we are obligated to do so.

To forget history is to unlearn any possible path forward, so I would like to begin this book and chapter with a very brief, in-exhaustive history of the gay rights movement within the United States.

1895-1930s

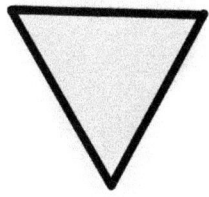

Alice Dunbar-Nelson, a biracial, bisexual woman, daughter of a Creole seaman and a Black seamstress, published her first collection of stories, poems, and essays, *Violets and*

Other Tales, in 1895. Dunbar-Nelson kept diaries for most of her adult life, and these were published in book form as *Give Us Each Day: The Diary of Alice Dunbar-Nelson* ninety years later, in 1985. She was candidly bisexual, biracial, and a woman. This, in the nineteenth century, was boundary-pushing, finally giving audiences an opportunity to read about non-hetero relationships. Some of her other works include a one-act play ("Mine Eyes Have Seen") and pieces selected for anthologies such as *Masterpieces of Negro Eloquence* and *Caroling Dusk: A Collection of African-American poets.*[15]

During World War I (1914-1918), large numbers of women were recruited into jobs vacated by men who had gone to fight. Within this group of voluntarily working women was a contingent of lesbians that formed the Women's Army Corps, which became a place where lesbian women could be out. After the war, many women—not just lesbians—refused to go back to traditional gender norms.[16]

In 1924, a German immigrant named Henry Gerber created the Society for Human Rights, the first documented gay rights organization in the United States.[17] This group, however, deliberately excluded bisexuals.[18] OUTMemphis: The LGBTQ+ Community Center of the Mid-South, an

---

15 Trish Bendix. "Queer Women History Forgot: Alice Dunbar-Nelson," *GO Magazine*, 22 March 2017.
16 "Lesbians, World War II and Beyond (Cont) · Lesbians in the Twentieth Century, 1900-1999," OutHistory.org, accessed May 1, 2020.
17 "LGBTQ Activism: The Henry Gerber House, Chicago, IL (US National Park Service)," National Park Service, accessed February 1, 2020.
18 Vern L. Bullough, *Before Stonewall: Activists for Gay and Lesbian Rights in Historical Context*, (Routledge), 27.

organization I frequented in undergrad, was born from this effort.[19] I imagine that while the Society for Human Rights set the original standard for queer organizations, OUTMemphis probably runs very differently and includes a much broader community of people than the Society.

Gerber had been inspired by the successes of the Scientific-Humanitarian Committee, a "homosexual emancipation" group in Germany, during his US Army service in World War I. His organization published the country's first gay-interest newsletter, "Friendship and Freedom."[20] But of course, in the 1920s, this was seen as a dangerous act. Police raided Gerber's home, arresting him and confiscating the papers. Gerber and his small group were jailed for three days, leading to the group's disbanding in 1925.[21] Gerber was at the forefront of a changing conversation among gays and lesbians that their problems were born from cultural, state-sanctioned oppression, not because of some negative value within their own sexual identities.

The newsletters and papers stolen by police prevented generations of gay activists from implementing Gerber's work, but now Gerber's Chicago house is a designated National Historic Landmark. He asserted that a shift in the way gay men and women viewed themselves was necessary for any progress to be made.[22]

---

19 "About Us" OUTMemphis, April 26, 2020.
20 "Gay Rights," History.com, Jun 28, 2017. Updated April 3, 2020.
21 Ibid.
22 Ibid.

Like many human rights movements, the gay rights fight ebbed and flowed in its publicity. The community remained mostly private, though people like English poet and author Radclyffe Hall continued to publish work on the topic of same-sex relationships. Hall wrote *The Well of Loneliness* in 1928, again asserting through her main characters that "sexual inversion" was natural.[23] We see the declaration of dignity in lines like, "Give us also the right to our existence."

During World War II, the Nazis held gay men in concentration camps. These men would be forced to wear the infamous pink triangle badge. This same sign was given to sexual predators, marking both separate groups as "deviant" and shrouding LGBTQ+ people in a criminal label they still must often fight, even in 2020.[24] Just as gay men were forced to wear pink triangles in the concentration camps, many lesbians were forced to wear black triangles, which signified that they, along with sex-workers, unmarried women, and women who did not want children, were "anti-social" and did not live according to the Nazis' ideals.[25] Trans people were likely also interned during this time, but since our current labels were not used back then, it would have been difficult to document these individuals and other members of the LGBTQ+ community.

---

23 Owen Keehnen, "Radclyffe Hall," Legacy Project Chicago, accessed February 1, 2020.
24 Matt Mullen, "The Pink Triangle: From Nazi Label to Symbol of Gay Pride," History.com, July 9, 2019.
25 "Symbols within the GSD Community," EIU Center for Gender and Diversity, accessed February 1, 2020.

1940-'50s

In 1948, in his book *Sexual Behavior in the Human Male*, Alfred Kinsey guessed that male sexual orientation lies on a continuum between exclusively homosexual to exclusively heterosexual. Only a few years later, he added *Sexual Behavior in the Human Female* to his author CV in 1953.[26] His work is debated in both the scientific and LGBTQ+ communities, but it gave us the popular Kinsey Scale, a graph of human sexuality that was hugely controversial at this time.

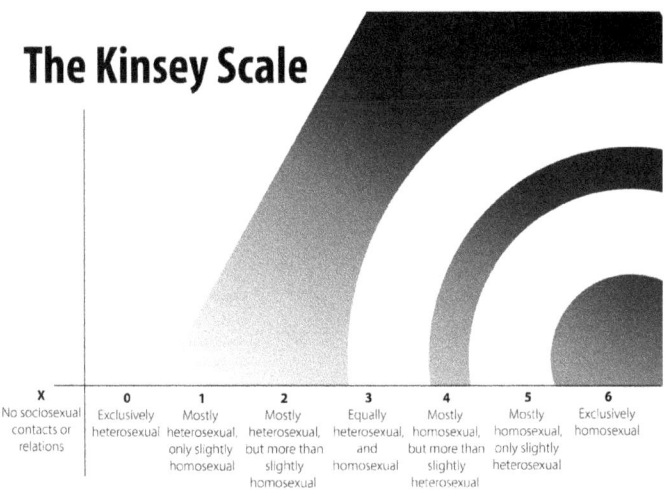

Other studies, however, have suggested that a scale isn't the best representation of sexuality. A group of distinct and meaningful categories may suit some people better.[27]

---

26 Sian Ferguson, "What's the Deal with the Kinsey Scale?" Healthline, January 29, 2020.
27 Samantha Allen, "Kinsey Was Wrong: Sexuality Isn't Fluid," The Daily Beast, April 13, 2017.

While it left out a large variety of other sexualities (assumed gender is binary and was not privy to the differences between romantic and sexual relationships), the Kinsey Scale recognized the fluidity that can come with sexuality. While no longer sleeping with men does not strip another man's potential bisexuality away, it gives him the right to move on the scale, to identify how *he* wants to move in any given relationship. This book will assert that this self-determined truth is hugely important, coming from self-reflection and evaluation and not simply from past experiences and other people's labels. Maybe that will be controversial too.

The question of choice in identity, to me, is difficult because this is often used against gay and lesbian individuals in arguments of morality policing (particularly by religious leaders and traditional, older generations). I do not believe this question is irrelevant, but because the answer is going to be *so* different for each individual, I think it deserves its own book. No one I know would actively choose a "lifestyle" that would put them in danger. Being outwardly gay or lesbian or trans can still be dangerous. Bi and pansexuality can also hold similar risks. Open LGBTQ+ presentation to the world in one or more categories may be unwelcomed in a number of spaces. That being said, my chosen partner is a cisgender (cis) straight male and, as a cis pan and bisexual woman, I have to recognize over and over again the privileges and benefits that came from what was ultimately a choice. All this is to say that I range from a two to four on the Kinsey scale on any given day and did not choose to have that range. While I see the groups not represented in this scale, it can be really convenient to understand others and myself with tools like this one.

1950s

In 1950, Harry Hay founded the Mattachine Foundation, one of the nation's first groups centering around gay rights advocacy. Members of this organization coined the term "homophile," which was considered less clinical and focused on sexual activity than "homosexual."[28] The Mattachine Foundation expanded after founding member Dale Jennings was arrested in 1952 for solicitation. After being set free due to a deadlocked jury, Jennings formed One, Inc., which welcomed women and published *ONE*, the country's first pro-gay magazine. This publication won a lawsuit against the US Post Office in 1954, when carriers declared the magazine "obscene" and refused to deliver it.[29]

The Mattachine Foundation morphed into the Mattachine Society, which began publishing the country's second gay publication, *The Mattachine Review,* in 1955. At the same cultural moment, lesbian couples in San Francisco founded an organization called the Daughters of Bilitis, which soon began publishing a newsletter called *The Ladder*, the first lesbian publication.[30] Both of the organizations were overwhelmingly white and middle-class in order to help the groups fulfill the requirements of respectability politics.[31]

While each era holds moments of celebration, elements of strife should also be mentioned. In 1952 the American

---

28 "Gay Rights," History.com, Jun 28, 2017 updated April 3, 2020.
29 Ibid.
30 Ibid.
31 Kent W. Peacock, "Race, the Homosexual, and the Mattachine Society of Washington, 1961–1970," *Journal of the History of Sexuality* 25, no. 2 (2016): 267-296.

Psychiatric Association listed homosexuality as a mental disorder, and President Dwight D. Eisenhower signed an executive order that banned gay people, guilty of "sexual perversion," from being able to earn and hold federal jobs. This ban choked any possibility of federal employment of openly queer employees for twenty years and significantly impacted the feelings of safety and citizenship within the LGBTQ+ community.[32]

BUILDING UP TO STONEWALL (1960-'70S)

In 1961, Illinois became the first state to decriminalize homosexuality, and a local TV station in California aired *The Rejected*, the first documentary about gay and lesbian individuals.[33]

In 1965, Dr. John Oliven, in his book *Sexual Hygiene and Pathology*, coined the term "transgender" to describe someone who, in his definition, was born in the body of the

---

32 "Gay Rights," History.com, Jun 28, 2017 updated April 3, 2020.
33 "Gay Rights," History.com, 2020.

incorrect sex. The more commonly agreed upon explanation for most transgender people in 2020 is something along the lines of "someone who doesn't identify with the gender they were assigned at birth."³⁴

Despite these small victories, LGBTQ+ individuals faced harassment and persecution, such as in bars and restaurants. In fact, gay men and women in New York City could not be served alcohol in public because, apparently, groups of gay people were "disorderly." Bartenders would deny drinks to patrons suspected of being gay or kick them out altogether based on their own internal biases and assumptions.³⁵ If they did serve drinks, gay folks were told not to socialize with others while drinking. All I can imagine is a 1960s Jill ("Yes, hi, hello, I am wearing flowered pants and lipstick on my cheeks, how do you do?") sitting alone at the bar with my bi/pansexual cocktail of choice (because everything I touch or look at immediately becomes gay) and avoiding verbal contact with any strangers on the off chance that maybe, just maybe, a woman would find my flower pants *particularly* dashing. This seems like a bad plan.

In 1966, members of the Mattachine Society in New York City staged a "sip-in"—because we love a good quip—in which they visited taverns, boasted their gayness, and quickly sued when turned away.³⁶ When denied service at the Greenwich

---

34 "Glossary of Terms | Human Rights Campaign," Human Rights Campaign. Accessed February 1, 2020.
35 "Gay Rights," History.com, Jun 28, 2017 updated April 3, 2020."
36 Thad Morgan. "The Gay 'Sip-In' that Drew from the Civil Rights Movement to Fight Discrimination," History.com, Jun 18, 2018 updated April 12, 2019.

Village tavern Julius in New York City, they gained lots of publicity that led to the removal of anti-gay liquor laws.[37]

In the same year, a group of trans women in San Francisco stood up to police inside Gene Compton's Cafeteria, an open-all-hours restaurant in the Tenderloin neighborhood and popular queer gathering spot.[38] Here a trans woman, fed up with the constant harassment and abuse from police, supposedly threw a cup of coffee in an officer's face, sparking an unprecedented instance of trans resistance to police violence. This event was nearly lost to history. Dr. Susan Stryker came across a brief mention of it in a news article at the Gay and Lesbian Historical Society archives in 1991 when she stumbled on a timeline of historic events that referenced an August 1966 event: "Drag queens protest police harassment at Compton's Cafeteria." She then, thankfully, kept digging.[39] With more research into LGBTQ+ history, we may find even more crucial events like this.

The erasure of Compton's Cafeteria from discussions of LGBTQ+ resistance is due, at least in part, to the exclusion of trans people from both the original Gay Rights Movement and Pride parades that followed. While Stonewall is the event cited by most LGBTQ+ people and allies alike as *the* event that propelled queer rights forward, Compton's Cafeteria is likely one of many crucial steps that have been overlooked by mainstream gay communities.

---

37 Morgan, 2019.
38 Sam Levin, "Compton's Cafeteria Riot: A Historic Act of Trans Resistance, Three Years before Stonewall," *The Guardian*, June 21, 2019.
39 Ibid.

STONEWALL AND BEYOND

The only cited LGBTQ+ specific event cited in many textbooks, **The Stonewall Riots**, occurred in 1969.

This gay club at the Stonewall Inn was a queer institution in Greenwich Village because it was big enough for many dancing bodies and inexpensive enough to welcome homeless youth. The resident trans women of color helped popularize this location.[40] Like many popular queer bars, Stonewall was owned by the mafia, who often bribed police to avoid conflict.[41]

But in the early morning of June 28, New York City police raided the establishment. The patrons there, tired of constant police harassment, began protests that lasted five days.[42] This event spurred a shift in the way LGBTQ+ people thought of themselves and were perceived by the public; they were more than a collection of people clandestinely hanging out with one another. They were an important group, a culture, who deserved political rights, social acceptance, and safety. Stonewall was a "coming out" for a community that fought

---

40 "Gay Rights," History.com, June 28, 2017 updated Apr 3, 2020.
41 Ibid.
42 Ibid.

for so long through the decades for recognition and rights, one that was finally being noticed.[43]

There are many legends about the Stonewall Uprising, but the most famous is that Marsha P. Johnson threw the first "shot glass heard around the world."[44] While the LGBTQ+ community credits Marsha P. Johnson with this legend, the accuracy of this statement is unconfirmed. Placing a riot's origin on one person removes the other LGBTQ+ people in the story in an effort to make the history easier to understand. Our common understanding of the uprising comes largely from oral histories that present conflicting stories about what happened at Stonewall. Both Johnson and Sylvia Rivera, a Latina transgender rights activist, denied being the first to fight back against the police during the uprising, but they, others, and the results of Stonewall are all worth celebrating.[45]

Shortly after Stonewall, some members of the Mattachine Society split off to form the Gay Liberation Front, a comparatively radical group that kept these events loud, public, and relevant to American conversation.[46]

After the riots, Marsha P. Johnson and Sylvia Rivera became notable organizers and participants at prominent gay rights protests. They also founded Street Transvestite Action

---

43 Mark Krone, "Stonewall Was Important but Not Because It Was First," FacingHistory.org, June 4, 2018.
44 Krone, 2018.
45 Chrysanthemum Tran, "When Remembering Stonewall, We Need to Listen to Those Who Were There," *Them*, 11 June 2020.
46 "Gay Rights," History.com, Jun 28, 2017 updated Apr 3, 2020.

Revolutionaries, or STAR, opening a house to shelter homeless LGBT youth—the first shelter to do so explicitly in the United States.[47]

These great works were overlooked as the movement grew, as some gay and lesbian activists wanted people like Johnson and Rivera out of their umbrella category in order to more efficiently claim that gay people are just like straight folks. This is not a supposition or an overstatement. .In the 2012 documentary "Pay It No Mind: The Life and Times of Marsha P. Johnson," you can see footage from a Pride March in 1973, when Rivera was repeatedly blocked from speaking and then booed off the stage for rightly saying, "If it wasn't for the drag queen, there would be no gay liberation movement. We're the front-liners."[48]

At the one-year anniversary of the Stonewall Riots in 1970, New York City community members marched through local streets to memorialize the event. This day, Christopher Street Liberation Day, is now considered to be the United States' first gay Pride parade. Activists in this group also claimed the WWII Pink Triangle as a symbol of Pride.[49]

Fifty years after Stonewall, in 2019, New York City finally paid tribute to Marsha P. Johnson and Sylvia Rivera, who had been pushed out of the original gay rights movement for being transgender, working class, and women of color. The

---

47 Gillian Brockell, "The transgender women at Stonewall were pushed out of the gay rights movement. Now they are getting a statue in New York," *The Washington Post*, June 12, 2019.
48 Brockell, 2019.
49 "Gay Rights," History.com, 2020.

city has decided to build a monument that will be the first in the world to honor two transgender individuals.⁵⁰

POST-STONEWALL

Stonewall hugely impacted the visibility of the LGBTQ+ community, giving them the momentum to push for even more rights. These events also allowed for a great, though imperfect, amount of new LGBTQ+ political and media representation.

Kathy Kozachenko won a seat to the Ann Arbor, Michigan, City Council in 1974, becoming the first out American to be elected to public office. In 1977, the New York Supreme Court ruled that Renée Richards, a transgender woman, could play against other women at the United States Open tennis tournament.⁵¹ In 1978, Harvey Milk campaigned on a wholly pro-gay rights platform, became the San Francisco city supervisor, and, with this title, the first openly gay man elected to a political office in California.⁵²

---

50 Gillian Brockell, "The transgender women at Stonewall were pushed out of the gay rights movement. Now they are getting a statue in New York." The Washington Post, June 12, 2019.
51 "Gay Rights," History.com, June 28, 2017 updated Apr 3, 2020.
52 Ibid.

Milk asked artist and gay rights activist Gilbert Baker to create a representation of the movement—the symbol of pride. Baker designed the rainbow flag, which he unveiled at a pride parade in 1978.[53] This symbol inspired different iterations of many more flags, including Daniel Quasar's trans and people-of-color inclusive flag.[54]

In 1979, more than 100,000 people took part in the first National March on Washington for Lesbian and Gay Rights.[55]

1980-'90s
So, in the '80s, we're loud and proud and demanding basic rights. The only other large LGBTQ+ related moment I can recall discussing in school other than Stonewall was the large outbreak of AIDS, though this disease also impacted many people outside of the LGBTQ+ community.

Still, Dianne Feinstein's budget for AIDS research and healthcare for San Francisco was larger than President Reagan's AIDS budget was for all of the United States. His proposed federal budget for 1986 actually called for a reduction in AIDS spending.[56]

Initially thought to be a rare type of pneumonia, researchers identified the cause of AIDS in 1984. They called it the human

---

53 Ibid.
54 Natashah Hitti, "Daniel Quasar Redesigns LGBT Rainbow Flag to Be More Inclusive," *Dezeen*, June 19, 2019.
55 Hitti, 2019.
56 Hank Plante, "Reagan's Legacy," *San Francisco AIDS Foundation*, Feb 10, 2011.

immunodeficiency virus, or HIV.[57] In 1985, the Food and Drug Administration licensed the first commercial blood test for HIV.[58] Two years later, the first antiretroviral medication for HIV, azidothymidine (AZT), became available to the public.[59] AIDS was not nationally covered by the media until the second National March on Washington for Lesbian and Gay Rights in 1987.[60] ACT UP (AIDS Coalition To Unleash Power), an advocacy group seeking to improve the lives of people with AIDS, took to news organizations to disentangle information regarding HIV and AIDS.[61] In 1988, The World Health Organization declared December 1 to be World AIDS Day, with over 100,000 reported cases of AIDS in the United States by 1990.[62]

George H.W. Bush's anti-gay policy had a lot to do with the lack of research and funding to learn about HIV and AIDS.[63] Though he signed the Americans with Disabilities Act, which protected people with HIV and AIDS from discrimination, and the Ryan White Comprehensive AIDS Resources Emergency Act, which provided funding for AIDS treatment, he still blocked people with HIV from entering the United States.[64] This made it incredibly difficult for an international AIDS conference planned within the US to take place.[65] The

---

57 "Gay Rights," History.com, June 28, 2017 updated Apr 3, 2020.
58 Ibid.
59 Ibid.
60 Ibid.
61 Ibid.
62 Ibid.
63 Ibid.
64 Camila Domonoske, "'Kinder Gentler Indifference': Activists Challenge George H.W. Bush's Record On AIDS," NPR.org, December 4, 2018.
65 Domonoske, 2018.

lack of urgency he felt toward the communities affected by HIV and AIDS is additionally proven by the fact that he only gave one speech on the topic.[66]

Despite the lack of government urgency, many movements called attention to HIV and AIDS. The NAMES Project Foundation, established in 1987, organized the creation of the AIDS Memorial Quilt, designed to foster healing and inspire action in the age of AIDS.[67] Die-Ins, frequently organized by ACT UP, helped to hold both the government and the medical community accountable.[68] You can find an HIV timeline in the Resources section of this book.

AIDS activist group ACT UP organized numerous protests on Wall Street in the 1980s. The group's tactics helped speed the process of finding an effective treatment for AIDS.

While many in America refused to acknowledge this epidemic, the community continued to push for rights and support. Only when it was revealed that AIDS affected more than just gay folks did policies finally began to shift. But by then an entire generation had been decimated, erasing many of the voices that had carried our history.

As the AIDS crisis devastated the LGBTQ+ community in the 1980s, Martha P. Johnson continued her work, marching with activist group ACT UP. After years of important work, however, her body was found floating in the Hudson River on

---

66 Ibid.
67 Domonoske, 2018.
68 "The AIDS Memorial Quilt: Learn More," AidsMemorial.org, November 20, 2019.

July 6, 1992.[69] While her death was quickly ruled a suicide, the documented cause was changed to an unexplained drowning after many protests. Johnson lived a life full of happiness and positivity but was repeatedly the victim of violent attacks. Many of her friends think she was murdered. Her case was reopened in 2012 and remains open today.[70] The play *Angels in America* by Tony Kushner opened on Broadway in 1993 and the musical *Rent* opened on Broadway in 1996. Both of these pieces won the Tony Award and the Pulitzer Prize Award and kept AIDS in mainstream theatrical conversations.

Thanks to the work of organizations like ACT UP, new infections in the United States, which had risen rapidly to a peak of 150,000 per year in the mid-1980s, declined to an estimated 40,000 per year in 1992.[71] But the view of AIDS as a "gay disease" still impacts the LGBTQ+ community today. Because of 2020's COVID-19, the Federal Drug Administration changed the recommended blood-donation deferral period of men who have slept with men from twelve months to three months, even though all blood is tested, verified, and checked before it's even passed on to those in need. The assumption that men who sleep with men somehow participate in riskier behavior is a bias that still hurts the community today.[72]

---

69 Nurith Aizenman, "How to Demand a Medical Breakthrough: Lessons from the AIDS Fight," NPR.org, February 9, 2019.
70 Gillian Brockell, "The transgender women at Stonewall were pushed out of the gay rights movement. Now they are getting a statue in New York," *The Washington Post.* June 12, 2019.
71 Brockwell, 2019.
72 "Coronavirus (COVID-19) Update: FDA Provides Updated Guidance to Address the Urgent Need for Blood During the Pandemic." US Food and Drug Administration, 2 April, 2020.

Also in 1992, the District of Columbia, following San Francisco, passed a law that allowed gay and lesbian couples to register as domestic partners, granting them some of the rights of marriage.[73] Bill Clinton campaigned with the promise to lift the ban against gays in the military. After failing to garner enough support, however, President Clinton passed the "Don't Ask, Don't Tell" (DADT) policy in 1993, which allowed gay men and women to serve in the military only if they kept their sexuality a secret, closeting them within their careers.[74] Despite this Don't Ask, Don't Tell policy, many men and women were still discharged on the grounds of their sexualities.[75]

In 1993, Hawaii's highest court ruled that a ban on gay marriage went against the state's constitution.[76] Yet state voters disagreed and voted to ban same-sex marriage in 1998.

During the unfolding of these events in Hawaii, federal lawmakers felt emboldened to pass the Defense of Marriage Act (DOMA), which Clinton signed into law in 1996.[77] This meant there would be no federal marriage benefits granted to same-sex couples, allowing states to refuse to recognize same-sex marriage certificates from other states.[78]

Somehow during the implementation of these discriminatory practices, violence against LGBTQ+ people was becoming

---

73 "HIV and AIDS—United States, 1981–2000," Center for Disease Control, June 1, 2001.
74 "Gay Rights," History.com, Jun 28, 2017 updated Apr 3, 2020.
75 Ibid.
76 Ibid.
77 Ibid.
78 Ibid.

intolerable. Shortly before DOMA's introduction, in 1994, a new anti-hate-crime law allowed judges to impose harsher sentences on criminals who were motivated by a victim's sexual orientation.[79]

AN IMPORTANT NOTE

So far, this history has taken on a pretty Western, colonial narrative. People whose sexual orientations and gender identities don't fit Western cis and heteronormative standards have lived on this continent long before the colonists arrived.

In 1993, Beverly Little Thunder and other LGBTQ+ Native American advocates met to discuss and produce resources for LGBTQ+ Native Americans.[80] At the time, anthropologists were using the word "berdache" to describe Native people who did not adhere to Western gender and sexual expectations.[81] This word translates to "boy prostitute" in Prussian. The group shared teachings from their different cultures and collaboratively decided on a new term, "two-spirit."[82]

In a HuffPost article, Little Thunder explained, "In many tribes if you are a two-spirit person, you embody both the masculine and the feminine."[83]

---

79 Ibid.
80 "Gay Rights," History.com, June 28, 2017 updated April 3, 2020.
81 Rebecca Nagle, "The Healing History of Two-Spirit, a Term That Gives LGBTQ Natives a Voice." HuffPost, June 30, 2018.
82 Nagle, 2018.
83 Ibid.

Currently there are more than forty regional two-spirit societies, supported by an international two-spirit council.[84] I want to be careful not to suggest that to be two-spirit is automatically to be trans. This term is often used as an overarching term for all LGBTQ+ Native Americans. Two-spirit is also pan-Indian, representing different cultures and tribes.[85] There is a huge diversity of tribes in the US, over 570 federally recognized, each with its own words and definitions for what people English-speakers call LGBTQ+.[86]

2000-2010s

The US Supreme Court, in *Lawrence v. Texas,* struck down the state's anti-sodomy law in 2003, effectively decriminalizing gay relationships nationwide.[87] Steps like these were huge because folks could no longer use legalities to support their homophobia.

In 2009, President Barack Obama signed the Matthew Shepard and James Byrd Jr. Hate Crimes Prevention Act into law, extending the reach of the 1998 law in response to Shepard's hate-driven torture and murder for being a gay man.[88] Further hate crimes continue to be perpetrated against the LGBTQ+ community, particularly against trans women of color. Some of the organizations that help bring justice to those harmed individuals are listed in the Resource List.

---

84 Ibid.
85 Nagle, 2018.
86 Nagle, 2018.
87 "Gay Rights," History.com, June 28, 2017 updated April 3, 2020.
88 Ibid.

In 2011, President Obama fulfilled a campaign promise to repeal Don't Ask, Don't Tell, after more than twelve thousand officers had been discharged from the military for making their sexuality known.[89]

A couple of years later, the Supreme Court ruled against Section 3 of the Defense of Marriage Act, no longer allowing the denial of federal benefits to married same-sex couples.[90] The Act was then finally overturned when the Supreme Court finally ruled that states could not ban same-sex marriage on June 26, 2015.[91] I was in Melbourne, Australia, on this day, and I remember many Facebook friends changing the filters on their profile images to rainbows. I recall the Australians around me stating how shocked they were that the States were "so far behind."

The Boy Scouts of America lifted its ban against openly gay leaders and employees the next day, taking a small second step after avoiding openly allowing gay boys in the organization until 2014.[92] In 2017, it reversed its ban against transgender boys, *finally* taking nods from the Girl Scouts of the USA, which had long been inclusive of LGBTQ+ leaders and children, accepted its first transgender Girl Scout in 2011.[93]

But on June 12, 2016, in an act of extreme terrorism, a gunman opened fire at Pulse, a gay nightclub in Orlando,

---

89   Ibid.
90   Ibid.
91   Ibid.
92   Ibid.
93   Ibid.

Florida, killing fifty people and wounding another fifty-three in the second-deadliest mass shooting in US history.[94] One Pulse Foundation has set up the Pulse Interim Memorial and is working to build a sanctuary of hope on the site of the nightclub.[95]

In the same month, the US military lifted its ban on allowing transgender people to serve openly, a month after Eric Fanning became the first openly gay secretary of a US military branch as the newest Secretary of the Army.[96]

Unfortunately, this new policy would not last long. In March 2018, President Donald Trump announced a new policy for the military that, again, banned most transgender people from serving.[97]

Danica Roem became the first transgender individual to serve in the Virginia House of Delegates in 2018, beating a longtime incumbent who was openly transphobic toward her in the election.[98] And in 2019, Pete Buttigieg was the first openly gay individual to run a major presidential campaign.[99]

---

94 Christopher Stults, "Perceptions of Safety Among LGBTQ People Following the 2016 Pulse Nightclub Shooting," *PubMed Central (PMC)*, 1 Sept. 2017.
95 "FAQs | OnePULSE Foundation," *OnePULSE Foundation*, 2 November, 2017.
96 "Gay Rights," History.com, Jun 28, 2017 updated April 3, 2020.
97 "Gay Rights," History.com, 2020.
98 Patrick Fort, "Election of Transgender Lawmaker in Virginia Makes History," NPR.org, November 8, 2017.
99 Reid Epstein and Trip Gabriel, "Pete Buttigieg Drops Out of Democratic Presidential Race," March 2, 2020.

2020s

So, here we are. Though LGBTQ+ Americans now have same-sex marriage rights, our work is far from finished.

Universal workplace anti-discrimination laws for LGBTQ+ Americans are still not consistent across the country.[100] An increasing number of "religious liberty" state laws allow businesses to deny service to LGBTQ+ individuals due to religious beliefs.[101] And I am exhausted by the arguments about the "bathroom laws" that prevent transgender individuals from safely using bathrooms without fear of verbal or physical attack.[102]

When I was first exposed to the idea of gay and lesbian orientations, these words were always hushed or used in a derogatory way. At four, I couldn't hold my friend's hands, her tiny fingers interlocking with mine, without some little boy calling us gay or even teachers telling us it wasn't appropriate. I didn't wholly realize until I was in high school that those prejudices had entered my own mind and were harming my ability to recognize my own desires without a heavy, unmoving press of shame in my chest. Additional identities entered my vocabulary in high school, but I didn't dare allow myself to consider that any of these new words—bisexual, pansexual, queer (along with the humorous and often debated "hetero-flexible")—as descriptions for myself. Recognizing this history helps me to understand why it can

---

100 "Gay Rights," History.com, Jun 28, 2017 updated April 3, 2020.
101 Ibid.
102 Ibid.

be so difficult to admit, even internally, that I have a place within this community.

Despite continuing hate crimes, under-representation, and denial, LGBTQ+ people continue to struggle for acceptance and equality while demanding respect and creating amazing works of art and of love. This progress is paved by our heroes—past, present, and future. Queer folks, currently, have to make the effort to learn the history of our elders if those stories are to live on. Without our intentional push for this documentation and representation, gaining the perspective that we aren't the first people to experience these things will continue to be an unnecessary challenge. Now we must find the best ways to continue this education, care for ourselves, for our community, and give ourselves the flexibility and strength for a progressive, inclusive future.

These history chapters were guided in large part by the research available from History.com's Gay Rights Archive. This resource is incredibly thorough and is worth exploring if you are interested in learning more of the LGBTQ+ stories that we don't learn formally in school.

MISTY: CALLED ME OUT

I have direct messaged (DMed) very few people on Twitter. In fact, as I write this story, I am only following ninety-four people. It actually took me an embarrassingly long time, a twenty-five-year-old woman getting a STEM degree, to figure out exactly how to send a Twitter direct message (there's a silly little letter icon, like on most platforms).

DMing Misty Gedlinske (she/her) after watching her TEDx talk, *Bisexuality: The Invisible Letter "B,"*[103] felt necessary,

---

103 Misty Gedlinske, "Bisexuality: The Invisible Letter 'B' | Misty Gedlinske | TEDxOshkosh," YouTube, n.d. youtube.com/watch.

though. She had called me out. We had never spoken and still have not exchanged very many words, but this talk threw me. She stated my fears so simply in seventeen minutes and fifteen seconds that I was teary-eyed and embarrassed by the end. It was all just *so* true. She also spoke with a hopefulness that I had yet to find in a vocal bisexual prior to viewing this video.

Misty compares bisexuality to a superpower. A superpower. Not an inconvenience, a scourge, or a turn-on. This is how she began the TEDx talk, and I was immediately drawn in, curious as to how this superpower would be explained. How would she pick apart the twist of shame I still feel in my stomach when talking about sexuality with straight people who don't know of my queerness? The concern I have around seeming too straight with my gay friends? Sadly, I have to report that she didn't solve these issues in seventeen minutes and fifteen seconds. What she did do, however, was empower me to really consider my sexuality. Reflect on it, actively archive my memories related to it, examine my feelings toward it, and become loud enough about it that young people with similar stories could seek me out. I have to say, that's probably more helpful in the long run than solving my insecurities about my orientation presentation. Feeling capable of being wholly myself was a far more useful way to use her TEDx talk.

This video came to me shortly before my wedding. I married my partner in July of 2019, sweating in the Nashville heat but thrilled anyway. Having a cis male partner kept me from feeling like I could fully take part in the LGBTQ+ groups on campus during my undergrad (we will talk about self-exclusion, do not fret!), and marrying him six years later felt like a million wins with one *teeny-tiny* loss. I knew that the privilege I had from people assuming I'm straight was now permanent. I'd have to verbally out myself with the people around me if I wanted to be honest about this aspect of my identity, and I knew that a lot of the time, other folks would feel like that was wasted information. Like Eric in Cassandra's story, I feared the people who knew this part of me would immediately dismiss it upon my marriage. I found myself bonding with my LGBTQ+ friends over women and gender nonbinary folks I found attractive more often in an attempt to *remind them* that I was still queer, when in reality I was just trying to reassure *myself*.

Misty called her wedding band a ring of power—one that increases invisibility. I didn't need a ring for the assumptions to come, but the two that sit on my finger now definitely don't scream, "I'm bi/pan/queer and that hasn't gone away because I fell in love!" This is probably a good thing because I don't think a screaming ring would fare well in most social situations.

But like she says, maintaining invisibility feels like a lie. Self-redirecting away from LGBTQ+ spaces for fear of contaminating the space with my willingness to pursue guys didn't protect my gay friends so much as it hurt me little by little, every day. I had become complicit in my own disappearance, contributing to **bisexual erasure** (when the legitimacy of bisexuality is questioned or denied) by allowing myself to become a victim of the problem. I know now that making space for myself doesn't need to impede on the group dynamic in discussing LGBTQ+ issues. I am just as passionate about accurate, inclusive representation as the next queer person. I can leverage my sexual orientation-presentation in an educational manner—correcting homophobic comments made before me by those mistaking me for a straight woman. In this way and more, bisexuality is a kind of superpower.

Misty additionally helped me become aware of a concern I did not know I held in my heart. I'd like to have children. On the stage she confidently stated, "I've been asked if my children know my orientation, or if I plan to tell them. They all know, in ways that we felt were appropriate to their respective ages, and the reason for that is I wanted them to understand that orientation is nothing shameful and that identity is not taboo."

I have never come out explicitly to anyone in my family, aside from the awkward beach conversation, though I have made social media posts centered around bisexuality and my own pride. I will go into the details of why I never felt comfortable discussing this with my family in later chapters, but I want to note here that I do not regret choosing my partner. In Gedlinske's words, "I picked a partner, not a side." While I can see people from my family naming my husband as proof that sexuality is chosen, I want to move forward without fear around fighting this idea. False binaries are another type of closet in which I refuse to sit any longer.

So why is the title of this chapter, "Misty: Called Me Out"? Well, to start with the basics, she shares my view of the definition of a bisexual person and spoke it publicly for others and me to find.

Bisexuals are people who experience some degree of romantic or sexual attraction to people of their same sex or gender as well as people of a different sex or gender. I've also used pansexual and queer to describe myself in the past, but these words were specifically used with disgust by the people around me while I grew up, so I am still working on my personal relationship with these words. Reclamation is a journey in which only some LGBTQ+ individuals choose to take part, and vocabulary's importance is discussed more throughout this book.

Gedlinske shared some frightening statistics. These were a huge reason why I decided I needed to write this book.

- Bisexual people make up 52 percent of the LGBTQ+ community but are six times more likely to hide their sexual orientation from friends and family than a gay or lesbian person.
- Only 44 percent of bisexual youth can confide in a trusted adult, and bisexual people have higher rates of substance abuse than their straight peers.
- More than one out of three of bisexual adults do not disclose their orientation to medical professionals, and many bisexual people have higher rates of anxiety and depression.
- Bisexuals are less likely to have relevant sex education than their straight peers.
- Bisexual women are 30 percent more likely to experience partner violence than their straight and lesbian counterparts.
- Forty percent of bisexual adults have considered or attempted suicide.[104]

---

104 "Understanding Issues Facing Bisexual Americans," Movement Advancement Project, BiNet USA, and Bisexual Resource Center, 2014.

I heard these statistics, hand on my keyboard and eyes on the TEDx YouTube channel, and felt that Misty was speaking directly to me. I have never disclosed my sexual orientation to an older family member. I had no mentors or trusted adults to talk to when I was a teenager. I have received small amounts of self-sought-out therapy to discuss my anxiety and depression around feeling unable to be wholly myself in my friend circles and larger communities. I am a small part of these statistics.

This conversation doesn't even begin to paint the larger picture of how beautiful the experience of bisexuality can be. So often (though, arguably, not often enough) we only talk about these numbers.

With this book, I have pulled together stories from people in the LGBTQ+ community that center on celebration. The individuals who have shared their stories with me are bi, pan, trans, ace, poly, and more. There will be mentions of disillusion, heartbreak, fear, and loss, but each story will center around a little victory. I am writing this selfishly, as a way to talk about the queer community in the ways I kept myself from doing in high school and college. I am also writing this so that if a young person finds it and is in the position I was when Misty Gedlinske called me out, they will have a resource to look to in order to build their own identity and wider community.

VISHAAL: OPPORTUNITY AND MEDIA REPRESENTATION

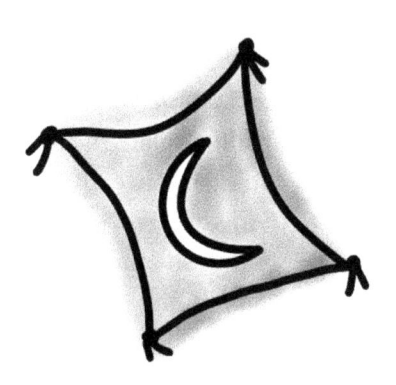

Vishaal Reddy (he/him), grew up with a strong imagination and people-centered mind in Johnson City, Tennessee. He realized he wanted to be a performer at the age of seven, and with his fictional online series, *Insomnia,* Vishaal is living out that goal. He tells hilariously strange stories centered around a character going through a queer, Indian-American identity crisis.

He also knew he was queer from a pretty young age but did not understand what it meant because he couldn't see himself within the boundaries that were always discussed. Vishaal told me, "When you aren't able to fit into one categorization of something, you tend to just pick one side of whatever the choice is and stick with it, but that doesn't necessarily work." So it wasn't until Vishaal went to high school that it became more clear to him that he was romantically interested in all sorts of people. By the time he got to college, he was ready to explore that side of himself and did. Once he moved to New York, he had completely accepted this identity. We joked about how everyone's timeline for acceptance is different and about how, luckily, different rates of acknowledgment are perfectly normal. The conversation reminded me much of my own realizations around my sexual orientation.

When I didn't fit under the lesbian label, I sort of floated around with knowledge that I wasn't straight, until I found a context in which to really explore the bi and pan part of my identity. It didn't "look good" in early high school when I was coming of age to claim that my attraction wasn't limited by a person's gender. That wasn't something I knew how to talk about properly until my junior or senior year. Even then, I held it to the edges of my mind until I couldn't avoid being in queer communities anymore. The realization itself wasn't particularly slow, but the acceptance and incorporation of acknowledgment into my daily life was definitely a multi-year process.

Vishaal's process began when he was younger, and he started to open his mind and heart to more than just women while watching television. "When I watched *Saved by the Bell*, I would watch *both* Kelly *and* Zach. I found myself thinking, 'Wait a second. I like both of these people. What are their stories? Let's dissect this.'"

Vishaal told me that these were the types of experiences that influenced his show, *Insomnia*.

Excitement and fear around discovering and misunderstanding oneself is a common recurrence in the show. His character, Nikhil, often finds himself in uncomfortable dating situations due to his dates' cultural biases or hetero-centric assumptions.

This tornado of feelings—empowerment, confusion, happiness, concern, and so on—is common within the queer experience because it is one always being questioned, if not mocked. It also comes from a serious lack of representation still occurring today. In fact, the limited series *Insomnia* was born out of a lack of not only South Asian identity but layered identity in media.

"I got frustrated with the lack of opportunity and the lack of care and intention around characters who are out there for us [both South Asian people and queer men]. I'm an actor first and just sort of started writing anything I could see myself in. I ended up with this concept about a guy with insomnia, who was also queer."

That wasn't the whole story behind the design of this character and what his day-to-day life looks like, however. "I got asked to be an escort [someone pays for their time and sometimes for sex], randomly. When I turned down the offer, this guy was kind of like, 'You people don't do this kind of thing.'" This would be an odd experience for anyone, but the sexualization and immediate DE-sexualization of the request was strange for Vishaal and gave him further fuel for *Insomnia*. "Kind of through that micro-aggression I realized I could turn the tables on any sort of stereotypes I was plagued with because we're not often sexualized as South Asian people. The sexually desirable people in Hollywood movies aren't South Asian. So I decided to play with that."

This wasn't the only element of stereotyping that Vishaal used the show to work against either. In fact, when building the crew, the diversity was deliberate. "Lots of people of color, lots of women. I think our top two positions were women-led, and nearly everyone are people of color. We have a joke that we had three straight white men on the set, which doesn't happen at all in Hollywood."

This type of representation in hiring is hugely important to increase diversity overall online, in film, and in television. According to a Hollywood Diversity Report from 2019, people of color made up only 19.8 percent of film leads, 12.6 percent of film directors, and 7.8 percent of film writers.[105]

The same study states that women make up 32.9 percent of film leads, 12.6 percent of film directors, and 12.6 percent of film writers.[106] Vishaal's purposeful deviation from the norm

---

105 Dr. Darnell Hunt, Dr. Ana-Christina Ramón, and Michael Tran, "Hollywood Diversity Report 2019: Old Story, New Beginning," (UCLA College of Social Sciences, 2019), 3-4.
106 "Hollywood Diversity Report 2019: Old Story, New Beginning," 3.

of hiring mostly white men lends itself to more inclusive, honest storytelling.

"I've always been very honest and open about the kind of work I want to do. I have no interest in creating work that doesn't challenge what people are thinking and saying. I just want to create a ton of South Asian characters and a body of work that I'm really proud of. I just want more of us to be seen in different ways." This was the manifesto behind the entire production, and it shows when you watch the series itself.

The only explicit representations Vishaal can remember seeing while growing up that felt closer to his own image were South Asian men in Bollywood movies. In fact, these films allowed Vishaal to fall entirely into his love for acting. He saw himself on screen for the first time, something he could not see consistently in any measure in Hollywood. He also found himself attracted to the clear, uninhibited presentation of many of the characters in Bollywood. "The theatricality in the drama, some of the storylines and the musical numbers made me realize the magic of musical theatre." This eventually led Vishaal into the world of theater in many of its forms, and he started doing plays and musicals. "That introduced me to a whole group of people who were very open and honest about who they were. Everyone seemed to also be just figuring it out, without pressures to be a certain way."

He mentioned a Bollywood movie that inspired him to want to become an actor, *Dil Tu Pagel Hai*. In another film, *Kal Ho Na Ho*, Vishaal remembered a side character having very obvious queer-suggestive traits. This element of the character was quickly passed over, dubbed as the strange one of the group but not really spoken about or very present. This character definitely wasn't celebrated. And again, this film isn't particularly old. There is so much to strive for in terms of representation for LGBTQ+ people in movies and television, and this needs to be more than side characters hinting at some difference from the people around them. This is why Vishaal does the work. This is why he is an actor and a storyteller.

And this is why he dove into a creative profession that isn't as lucrative for him as it is for most straight, white men. The realization that he will have to be a large part of the push for more diversity in this field gives him even more passion for the work, especially on the harder days. He asserted to me that

> "Anyone who's marginalized, who does something that is outside the box, does not go into it because they think it's going to be something that's going to make life easier. We're doing it because we want to say something. I am at my most authentic self now, and most people, honestly, just go with it."

Most people just go with it. This is a lesson I hope to take with me forever because it was something I so vividly felt while watching *Insomnia*.

Vishaal's advice for anyone struggling to find stories that are familiar to them is to really scour social media. It may not feel like direct contact, but any sort of Instagram account or message board that can feel helpful is worth keeping on-hand, particularly if you don't have that representation in your real life. "Look out in your community. Wherever you are, there are people who are like-minded and who do share similar interests. If you're able to feel like you're safe and can do it, create it."

Vishaal found a lot of community in the arts and through reading. Formulating his own opinions was a stepping stone, digesting everything he could to figure out what he needed from a community and also what he could give. And through his work with *Insomnia,* there was a lot of reward for the work.

"We had our big premiere in Brooklyn. And I remember sitting there with three hundred people looking at me after we'd watched the show." Vishaal recalls crying because of the number of people and their support. "They all just came to watch this show about a queer Indian kid navigating life and also messing up. And he's also a sex worker. He's messy. And he's funny." His character is complicated, and Vishaal had an audience for him, an audience that wanted to have conversations about *Insomnia* and all its layers of empowerment and truth. "And that… that gave me joy."

We deserve this joy. As LGBTQ+ people, we're seeing more musicians, actors, artists, and digital media content creators come out more often, but I don't think it quite reflects the way it should on mainstream media yet. There are still too many shows with a single, cisgender, gay best friend who solely exists to serve the main character, too many examples of one gay couple who has to stand in for an entire community. I remember watching *Degrassi* and feeling queasy when a female character wanting to explore her sexual preferences toward women used a trans man to experiment with these desires, and it all got very dramatic and confusing.

Without claiming that these types of stories do not occur in real life, I want to vouch for better, more positive, *joyful* storytelling. I want more of the kind of storytelling I got to experience while binging the entirety of *Schitt's Creek* with its heartwarming finale and end-of-series special within one year. That was the first show I'd seen that prioritized joyful depictions of LGBTQ+ relationships and did not use homophobia as a major plot point.

We deserve more shows like *Brooklyn Nine-Nine*, a wonderful comedy created by Andy Samberg. His character, Jake Peralta, repeatedly embarrasses himself and eventually befriends Captain Raymond Holt (Andre Braugher), a masculine, black man in a position of authority whom the show makes a point to celebrate as the first openly gay officer in the precinct. Instead of making his queerness the butt of jokes, *Brooklyn Nine-Nine* made the ignorance surrounding it the punch line. Even better, Holt isn't the only LGBTQ+ character. Rosa (Stephanie Beatriz, who is actually bisexual herself), the show's resident badass, comes out as bisexual in the show's one-hundredth episode.[107] And it's not a one-and-

---

107 Stephanie Beatriz, "Stephanie Beatriz Is Bi and Proud as Hell," *GQ*, June 21, 2020.

done. Her character discusses family matters, celebrations, and breakups in later episodes, reminding viewers of her identity and normalizing it well.

Netflix's original show *Sex Education* presents the gay best friend (GBF) trope in a new, important way. This GBF character, Eric, gets his own storylines, his own life. Ola, the love interest of the main character, discovers herself to be pansexual and takes an online quiz to confirm her suspicions about her sexuality—something I think most LGBTQ+ people can admit to doing just for fun at one point or another. The show even mentions asexuality, a topic I personally had never seen covered in film or television, with the line, "Sex doesn't make us whole, so how could you ever be broken?"

One of the biggest takeaways any TV executive or writer who may happen to pick up this book can learn from these shows is that relieving the burden of a single queer character can make a huge difference to the authenticity of the stories. Multiple, diverse queer characters who carry their own storylines are necessary to garner respect in representation. Audiences won't assume you're using your one queer character as a vehicle to represent all LGBTQ+ people if you actually have more than one character. It's a simple solve, really.

I do need to note, too, that similar to people playing characters not within their own racial identity or disability status, there are a number of examples of transgender characters played by cisgender actors. Scarlett Johansson, a cisgender white woman, was invited to play both an Asian character and a trans character in different films. We see this repeatedly in examples of movies and shows that include Jeffrey

Tambor, Jared Leto, and Felicity Huffman.[108] It's long past time to offer trans people these opportunities.

In popular media now, we have examples of completely different mindsets around pressures and obligations to be out. We need better characters in television and film, but also a more open mindset when it comes to the real lives of celebrities.

Harry Styles, originally known for his part in the band One Direction, for example, has frequently hinted at having a queer identity in his recent music videos and in speaking with press. In an interview with *The Guardian* in 2019, he said, "What I would say, about the whole being-asked-about-my-sexuality thing—this is a job where you might get asked. And to complain about it, to say you hate it, and still do the job, that's just silly. You respect that someone's going to ask. And you hope that they respect that they might not get an answer."[109]

Janelle Monáe, in a *Rolling Stone* article in 2018, stated "Being a queer black woman in America, someone who has been in relationships with both men and women—I consider myself to be a free-ass motherfucker." Though she initially identified as bisexual, she later clarified, "but then later I read about pansexuality and was like, 'Oh, these are things that I identify with too.' I'm open to learning more about who I am."[110]

---

108 *Transparent* 1-5. Amazon Prime, 2015.; *Dallas Buyers Club*. Focus Features, 2013.; *Transamerica*. ⊠Belladonna Productions, 2005.
109 Tom Lamont, "Harry Styles: 'I'm Not Just Sprinkling in Sexual Ambiguity to Be Interesting,'" *The Guardian*, December 15, 2019.
110 Brittany Spanos, "Janelle Monáe Frees Herself," *Rolling Stone*, June 25, 2018.

These two artists both sit on differing sides of a clarity struggle that many LGBTQ+ fans find irritating. Demi Lovato's documentary shows her swiping through both men and women on Tinder, and she states that she is more interested in personal connection. This, to many, would suggest she's pansexual. She confirmed this with *PinkNews*, saying, "I'm very fluid, and I think love is love. You can find it in any gender. I like the freedom of being able to flirt with whoever I want."[111] While audiences really do not have personal stakes or rights to the timelines of famous peoples' coming out stories, many still seem to put on that pressure. These "sides," celebrities-should-be-out versus celebrities-deserve-privacy-too aren't a binary either. Everyone has a different opinion and they all vary, even those who are ostensibly "on the same side." In talking about each perspective, we at least open an opportunity for some level of understanding.

And in many ways a lot of privilege is involved with who can "dangle" their potential queer sexuality in front of an audience for profit and who cannot. Freddie Mercury's story is often straight-washed, like in *Bohemian Rhapsody*, as he was never able to be straightforward about his sexual preferences publicly. David Bowie is often tokenized as strictly gay, though he, at least at one point, identified as bisexual, and was able to do so with the cushion of a wife and child.[112], [113]

---

111 Josh Jackman, "Demi Lovato Has Revealed the Truth about Her Sexuality," *PinkNews*, June 26, 2019.
112 *Bohemian Rhapsody*. Twentieth Century Fox Home Entertainment, 2019.
113 Nick Levine, "Who Was the Real Freddie Mercury?" *BBC*, October 11, 2019.

We are also in a time where we see the rise of poets like Saeed Jones, who told the Poetry Foundation, "I'm obsessed with manhood as a brutal and artful performance. My mind always finds its way back to the crossroad where sex, race, and power collide."

LGBTQ+ artists are recognizing their layered identities, pushing back against the idea of the cis white gay as the spokes-type for the community. And if you type in LGBTQ+ keywords on YouTube and don't have on any sort of restrictions, you can find examples of coming out videos, It Gets Better Project short films, and, best of all in my opinion, video blogs of a huge range of LGBTQ+ people just living their lives and finding joy in their day-to-day experiences. Access to this kind of representation made a huge difference in my own self-discovery, and the push for better depictions of diverse queer perspectives, like Vishaal's *Insomnia*, will continue to widen that reach.

ROBYN: VULNERABILITY TO ACTIVISM

Robyn Ochs (she/her and they/them) realized she was bisexual after falling head over heels in love with her female housemate, Miranda.* She described this love as "*West Side Story* level," a Tony and Maria kind of crush. She was obsessed.

If the two were in a room full of people, Robyn always knew exactly where Miranda was; she could *feel* her presence. She experienced this crush during the first month of college and went through the internal process of asking herself whether or not she was a lesbian.

"The way I was understanding it was that a lesbian was someone who was attracted to women but who wasn't attracted to men. I knew I was attracted to this woman. So, I did an inventory of my previous attraction history toward men to figure out if these crushes and emotions were just born from performative heteronormativity. But it didn't take me very much revealing to realize that they were real," Robyn remembers.

In her journey with Miranda, Robyn also considered whether she was really straight and that maybe this crush was a one-off, the exception that proves the rule, a blip on the radar. She thought maybe if she didn't act on these feelings, this emotional pull toward Miranda, they would go away. But they persisted. Robyn joked, in fact, that she still has a crush on this woman today. The tie was not severed by inaction or time.

"Except that the me-now doesn't have a crush on the her-now. The then-me still has a crush on the then-her. It's been a part of my life for forty years," she laughed.

I made a point to reach out to Robyn, a celebrated bisexual activist, because I knew she'd help me acknowledge the weirdness I felt around switching between the terms "bisexual" and "pansexual," depending on my audience. Apparently, this isn't an uncommon experience. Many of the bi and pansexual people I have spoken with use these terms interchangeably. For many people, it's easier to describe themselves as "bisexual" to people outside of the community, because "pansexual" is, somehow, still an emerging term. But even within the LGBTQ+ community, there is debate around these two terms.

The jargon within the community is something that LGBTQ+ allies have complained about, and it genuinely can be difficult to keep up when there are disagreements. Respect is the true name of the game, though, and Robyn confirmed that even agreed-upon definitions are often flawed, anyway. Vocabulary familiarity is helpful, but what is most important for both the LGBTQ+ community and its allies is a willingness to listen openly without becoming defensive when one doesn't adhere to your own standards or labels.

"My definition of bisexuality is very different from the one you will find in *Merriam Webster*. In fact, we are working currently with *Merriam Webster* to try to get them to update the definition they use to sync with current usage," Robyn told me, reminding me that very few things in this world are permanent, especially in regards to language.

Currently, *Merriam Webster* defines bisexuality as "of, relating to, or characterized by sexual or romantic attraction to both men and women." But most bisexuals don't think of themselves that way. This dictionary definition is often weaponized to call bisexuality binary and oppressive (which is likely *sometimes* true, but is not inherent) in a world where more and more people are coming out as existing outside the binary of male and female on the spectrum of gender.

I particularly enjoy the Gender Elephant from the Canadian Centre for Gender and Sexual Diversity to help people new to these conversations understand the differences between sex, gender, expression, and physical and romantic attraction.[114]

The Gender Elephant

THE CANADIAN CENTRE FOR GENDER + SEXUAL DIVERSITY / LE CENTRE CANADIEN DE LA DIVERSITÉ DES GENRES + DE LA SEXUALITÉ

Gender Identity
- Female/Woman/Girl
- Male/Man/Boy
- Other Gender(s)

Gender Expression
- Masculine
- Feminine
- Other

Sex Assigned at Birth
- Female
- Other/Intersex
- Male

Physically Attracted to
- Men
- Women
- Other Gender(s)

Emotionally Attracted to
- Men
- Women
- Other Gender(s)

To learn more, go to ccgsd-ccdgs.org

inspired by TSER

In Robyn's definition, one with which I identify, a bisexual individual is someone who is attracted to their same gender *and* other genders. Robyn calls herself bisexual because she acknowledges within herself "the potential to be attracted, romantically or sexually, to people of more than one gender, not necessarily at the same time, in the same way, or to the same degree."

As our understanding of gender has evolved, so have the terms and definitions people use within and outside of the LGBTQ+

---

114 "The Gender Elephant," CCGSD, July 25, 2018.

community. People who are active in the bisexual community have adapted to that new understanding. For these folks, the "bi" in bisexual refers not to men and women but rather to an individual's own gender and any different gender.

Robyn explained that if one hundred bisexual people were asked to define that term, there would be a variety of responses. If we required 100 percent consensus on terminology in order to move forward, we would never move forward. One of the fun quirks about identity is that it's subjective. Its individual. It's our own.

"It's a combination of our own understandings of ourselves and community negotiation," Robyn said. "I've learned that if somebody shares an identity with me, if I really want to understand who that person is, the first thing I should do is thank them for sharing their identity because that is a gift. Then, I want to ask them if they will be willing to tell me more about what it means to them to use that term."

When I call myself bi, this may not be true to me in the same exact way it is true to Robyn. And vice-versa. As Robyn explains it,

> "A sign on the door is just a sign on the door, but it doesn't really tell us very much about what's behind it."

We so often get caught up in who's using a word improperly and who's using it properly, but I don't think those are answerable questions. *Rolling Stone* even interviewed queer activist and *Younger* star Nico Tortorella about it, where he mentioned the ways in which these terms are loaded, saying, "In the [queer] movement right now, we have a tendency of getting hung on specific words rather than the person... I'm really attracted to this idea that it doesn't have to be one thing."[115]

I would say I look forward to the days when I don't come across Reddit threads aching to try to disprove that bisexuals are all trans-exclusionary, but I do not actually think this will happen.[116] People will continue to find reasons to argue one way or another. My definition matters in my own life and the same is true for every other LGBTQ+ label. I do hope, though, that more and more people, including those who define bisexuality differently than I do, will make an effort to include our trans and gender nonbinary friends.

Robyn put it in a way I think is very useful when she said, "Imagine if we could take all that formidable energy that gets wasted in these debates and instead use it to hold space for all of us? We would be much better served."

Robyn's primary identity in terms of sexuality is bisexual, but she also uses "pansexual" and "queer." Her primary pronoun is "she," but Robyn is also comfortable with "they." In 2019, *Merriam Webster* added "they" to the dictionary as a

---

[115] Zachary Zane, "What's the Real Difference between Bi- and Pansexual?" *Rolling Stone*, October 4, 2019.

[116] "To All the People Wondering Whether Bi Is Trans Exclusionary: LEARN OUR HISTORY, FFS: Bisexual," Reddit.com, accessed February 1, 2020.

singular pronoun.[117] Consider carrying a copy of the Gender Elephant in your pocket (metaphorically or literally, whatever will help you remember—it's very cute!) and be actively sensitive to people's pronoun usage when you meet new people and quickly but genuinely apologize for any mistakes.

Robyn described the "2020 hindsight game" to me, a process many queer people go through, looking into our pasts to find clues and hints pointing to early indications of our sexuality or gender.

"There were clues and flashing lights and sirens and fireworks, none of which I saw at the time. I think I had my first crush on a girl when I was eight. My second crush on a girl happened from ages ten to sixteen, but again, I didn't see it as a crush. I just thought that she was perfect. I wanted to be her best friend more than I wanted life."

While Robyn can point to these feelings today as indicators, the still-prevalent views of same-gender partnerships as abnormal continue to prevent young people from making these connections. I, myself, have had plenty of crushes on people from various genders, but I was not able to put words to these feelings until I was fifteen because I didn't know these relationships were a viable, healthy option. I had no examples of women in romantic partnerships in my life, no examples of people identifying as a gender they weren't assigned at birth, and definitely no space to explore these ideas safely.

---

117 "Singular 'They,'" *Merriam-Webster*, accessed February 1, 2020.

These environmental factors put walls up in my own head, and it seems this happened to Robyn as well. "I guess I wasn't ready to notice," Robyn said. "I never told Miranda I was attracted to her. It was probably very obvious, but we never talked about it and still have not to this day. I was terrified."

She was terrified despite having gay and lesbian role models. She did not know anyone who identified as bisexual, and this lack of representation silenced her for a period of time. Another person opening up to Robyn allowed her to begin vocalizing this identity.

"When I was twenty-three, two years after college, I was working in a group home, and part of my job was doing overnight shifts. One night, my coworker sat me down and said, 'Robyn, I want to talk to you. There's something I want to tell you.' And I said, 'Sure, what's up?' and she said to me, 'I'm bisexual.'" Robyn was so excited that she immediately yelled out, "Me too!" It was the first time she had ever said it out loud, a gift she had found through her coworker's vulnerability.

"I experienced a profound sense of relief. I exhaled deeply for the first time in five years. And that opened the door for me to start telling other people. That simple act allowed me to start having conversations with friends and with family members."

Robyn moved to Boston, where she found a local feminist newspaper called *Equal Times*. While looking through their calendar listings, she found a weekly discussion group at the Women's Center called Women's Rap. Each week they focused on a different topic, but bisexuality happened to be the topic of the week when Robyn discovered the group. She happily found herself in a space where, out of the twenty women in the room, nineteen identified as bisexual. "Before this, I wasn't even sure there were nineteen bisexual people in the whole world."

Eight of these women, including Robyn, became the BiVocals, an activist group that met monthly for ten years. Together they created a space where their bisexual identity was not under attack or questioned but assumed and normalized. Unfortunately, this acceptance is not always the case in the larger LGBTQ+ community.

"On April 1, the local paper's *Gay Community News* section published their April Fools edition, which was an annual occurrence. And in this issue, they had an ad for 'Bisexuality insurance.' It was an ad in which one woman says to the other, 'I'm sorry. I'm leaving you for a man,' and then something like, 'Has this ever happened to you? You need bisexuality insurance. Protect yourself from up to two lovers simultaneously…' or something like that. We were not amused."

The group immediately wrote a letter to the paper, publishing their response to this in-community bias. One line Robyn remembers specifically stated, "Some of us are monogamous. Some of us are **polyamorous**.[118] Some of us are celibate. And some of us are assholes, just like some lesbians." This was the group's first act of overt bisexual activism. The BiVocals started The Bisexual Women's Network and organized more broadly, starting *Bi Women Quarterly*,

---

118 Ashley Mardell, *The ABC's of LGBT+*, (Mango Media Inc, 2016.), 12.

a grassroots publication. Robyn ended up co-founding the Bisexual Resource Center, which remains an active non-profit organization. While much of Robyn's career has been built by her part in these organizations, she serves as a great example of someone who also works to be an ally to various communities.

"Bisexuality is not the issue that I care about more than any other issue. I care about a large number of things: racism, the relentless destruction of the environment, domestic violence in all of its forms. I would like to change our educational systems so that people are actually supported. I do a large number of different kinds of advocacy." Robyn's work is highly intersectional and inclusive, but when she was first getting involved, bisexual activism was not garnering a lot of attention. She has figured out a way to merge her passions, selling merchandise that—in addition to funding *Bi Women Quarterly*—fuels donations to Black Lives Matter.

In acknowledging that we are all multi-dimensional, layered, and able to hold multiple forces in our hearts, Robyn serves as an example of someone who can recognize her privileged identities while simultaneously fighting for her marginalized ones. She also makes sure that if she's on a panel, the panelists aren't all white. If they are, she offers to volunteer her slot to someone not yet represented and to help find someone for the panel. This type of ally-ship is worth reflecting upon and implementing. In her ally-ship Robyn has found relief from shame and exclusion in her own identities. She taught me that when we talk about ourselves from a place of shame and discomfort, those things come through in our relationships with other people. Though it is not our fault that we often speak in this negative way, it does make it harder for other people to take us seriously.

I remember coming out to my husband as if it was some sort of apology. My tone implied that it would be an inconvenience to our relationship. I was scared that he would not accept this part of me. I, of course, was incorrect. I wouldn't have married him, or even dated him for another second, had he been unaccepting, but I had sat in that fear for weeks before allowing him into this part of my life. I wish I had expected the respect he gave my honestly. I am much better at these conversations now and hope to pass this idea to anyone reading: You deserve to be heard, to have space, and to feel respected.

STACY: Q AND OC

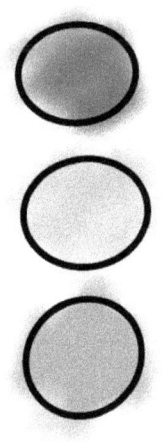

"I was out with friends at a very random house party. I found myself alone but open to meeting new people. I ended up speaking with this person, and we *clicked* instantly. I thought we'd be immediate friends. It didn't dawn on me during that conversation, but they had been suggesting we be more than that." Even after this person asked for her number, Stacy* (she/her) still didn't realize this person had been flirting with her. She had never been in a place where someone who wasn't a man had the opportunity to strike up a romantic conversation. Without prior knowledge of queer community, Stacy had to take a minute to understand what was happening, but she was into it.

Queer community can be found without needing to seek groups and organizations with that specific label. Stacy accidentally found exactly the type of friend-group she needed, but her story helps depict why LGBTQ+ representation is *crucial*. We need multiple examples of the ways queer folks can present themselves because seeing those variances almost grants us the *permission* we need to question our own romantic preferences. We often want representatives who look like us, grew up in similar communities, and face familiar challenges.

According to the Human Rights Campaign:

- Over 1 million LGBTQ+ African Americans currently live in the United States.
- Approximately 3.7 percent of all African American people identify as LGBTQ+.
- LGBTQ+ African Americans are disproportionately young and disproportionately female.
- Nearly one-third of all African American same-sex couples are raising children.[119]

More broadly, 39 percent of LGBTQ+ adults in the United States identify as people of color, including 15 percent who identify as the nonbinary Latinx, 11 percent as Black, 2 percent

---

119 "Being African American & LGBTQ: An Introduction," Human Rights Campaign, accessed February 1, 2020.

as Asian Pacific Islander, and 1 percent as Native American. With increasing acceptance of LGBTQ+ people generationally, younger folks, including those of color, are more likely to be out as LGBTQ+. During our LGBTQ+ Revolution 2.0, we need to respond and adapt to a new generation in the US that is more diverse than any previous generation in terms of race, sexual orientation, and gender identity, and this change starts with vocal grassroots organizers like Stacy.[120]

Stacy comes from a small town in Ohio—a place she described as conservative. It was the type of place to grow up where, even when not explicitly told that being "different" was bad, those implications hung heavily like humidity in the air. The statistics above were available to her online, but finding queer community in real life seemed like a daunting task.

Stacy identifies as bisexual and has successfully built a Black, queer community for herself made up of organizers found individually, all connecting either through friends or through grassroots operations. I find Stacy's story compelling because, in some ways, it mirrors my own, testing out LGBTQ+ language with people one-on-one over time to determine my own level of safety in different contexts. Fears around how her sexuality might impact her career prevented Stacy from looking inward to acknowledge her sexuality, which made the process of putting a name to it only more difficult.

Luckily, Stacy was able to join a Black-centered organization after moving out of her home town, where she started to meet people and learn more about her queer identity. Through this

---

120 "People of Color," LGBTQ Funders, accessed February 1, 2020.

organization, Black queer community became more substantial, real, and more than just numbers on a website. She found friendship and, even more importantly, space to allow herself to *be* herself. By seeking out community, Stacy was able to expand her network, opening herself up to making connections that could include folks identifying as both Black and LGBTQ+. She didn't need to announce being LGBTQ+, wear a rainbow name-tag, or use unsubstantiated stereotyping to find queer friends. They came out to her during naturally flowing conversations about other topics like politics, weekend events, favorite television shows, and music.

Over the phone, Stacy kept bringing up the idea of *permission*. Stacy found permission in this group of people who, like her, were figuring out how to layer their identities in a way that made sense to them. She found permission to change her straight-identity to a queer one. She needed a push and a safe place to really consider *why* she'd spoken of herself in a particular way for most of her life and whether or not she thought she could feasibly start recognizing this part of her story.

The house party where Stacy totally overlooked the flirtation in her conversation with a stranger may have gone differently had she found this community sooner, but she did verbalize something to me that comes up often, particularly with women. We are *constantly* complimenting each other to a point where it can sometimes be hard to tell where the line is between platonic conversation and flirting. This is so much easier to differentiate once we are out and LGBTQ+ and exploring with confidence, but I can recall flirting with women long before I actually recognized what I was doing. Coming to an understanding of one's bisexuality, particularly when attraction to the heteronormative gender is still present, can take a long time.

The stranger at the party found Stacy again later, right before she was about to leave, and asked her to dance.

"I was like, 'Okay, whatever.' But then I felt it in my kidney, my liver. I remember the moment." The stranger had gotten very close to Stacy's face and she froze, not knowing what to do with her body, her hands, her expression. Stacy panicked and left quickly, later torturing herself, overanalyzing every little element of the interaction.

"I knew I was into it, but I wasn't ready."

I want to assert here that everyone has a right to be out or not, to take as much time as they need to explore their gender and sexual and romantic identities, and to define these things for themselves. There isn't a particular timeline everyone is on together and, particularly for folks who don't have their own identities represented, patience and grace are key.

This moment at the house party was frustrating, but Stacy noted it as hugely important for her to recognize all types of attraction she feels now. Heteronormativity gives us all a weirdly shielded vision that can sometimes only be cleared by another person's time and attention. The organization Stacy joined helped her find those things. There, she was able to have conversations about how bisexuality is so often hyper-sexualized that there are debates surrounding cisgender women performing bisexuality solely for the pleasure of men. These were the types of fears and curiosities she'd never had the opportunity to vocalize before.

This hyper-sexualization is hugely distracting for young people trying to determine their preferences. It can be impossible to feel comfortable exploring these feelings when you can easily be written off as a faker, someone just wanting to seem interesting and garner attention. Stacy stressed to me that she was aware of all of these colliding ideas going on in her mind, and she recognized them as untrue and unhelpful, but she found them really difficult to push past, anyway. Part of celebrating LGBTQ+ identity is acknowledging the sticky parts, the pieces we still need to move through because that hard work lends itself to growth and self-expression. Challenging conversations and community helped Stacy to finally want to come out with her bisexuality, years after the party, sharing publicly on National Coming Out Day.

National Coming Out Day is an annual LGBTQ+ awareness day observed on October 11, celebrating and encouraging people who are "coming out of the closet." Stacy made a social media post on this day for multiple reasons, possibly the most important of which was to avoid needing to have the conversation with her family more than once. She did grow up in a conservative community, and prioritizing her own convenience over potentially damaging individual conversations was an act of self-care that I admire. "I'd much rather they just see it on the internet than get to push back against it individually."

Her parents' initial reaction was one of kind dismissal. They assumed she'd just been in the "big city," away from home, for too long. Their second reaction was to ask her to bring the woman she was seeing home, which was a nice gesture but "was extra awkward because I was still very much single. They wanted to see me partnered and I had to tell them I wasn't at that point, either."

I doubt the trope of parents just wanting to see their kids partnered and familied-up will ever leave our mainstream cultural lexicon, but it felt good to hear Stacy joking about this. She dealt with the older family members and, by being out, was able to stand as a strong mentor to her younger sister when she also came out as bisexual. Stacy proudly told me, "I'm the oldest and getting to defend her was and remains important to me."

In my own multi-faceted identity as someone who was raised in the Catholic church, I decided early on that I didn't want to have to come out to my family unless I had someone specific to bring home. I did not want a huge conversation. I certainly did not want multiple huge conversations. I had felt enough discomfort from my tale from the beach that I truly felt that, while I would always be loved, I would not get the kind of verbal support I would need. If anything, I thought I would be gossiped about and laughed at. That could still happen now, particularly with the publishing of this book, but I now have Stacy as an example of strength and resilience. Stacy accidentally found queer community by intentionally working to celebrate her other identities, which, to me, is a cool way to take away some pressure and forge additional representation.

Stacy's Black LGBTQ+ peers helped her to reflect on who she wanted to be, and that power is worth seeking.

RIVER:
ASEXUAL IDENTITY

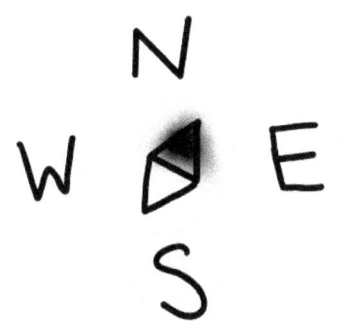

—

```
      N
W    ◇    E
      S
```

River (they/them) sometimes feels excluded from the LGBTQ+ community because of a stereotype that the community is hyper sexual. This gross bias likely comes from a variety of unreliable sources, but most people point to the 1960s propaganda films that labeled gay men as sexual predators, the Hays Code that predated the MPAA and banned homosexuality as a form of "sexual perversion" from being in films well into the 1960s, and fearmongering arguments against transgender bathroom bills. Our cis-heterosexist society often defines the LGBTQ+ community solely based on sex.[121]

But the LGBTQ+ community does not deserve this disgusting rhetoric, and the resulting systems left for LGBTQ+ individuals to find one another—often bars or dating apps—can leave queer people who do not prioritize sex out of the conversation.

River identifies as **ace (asexual)**, which is commonly used by people who define this element of their identity as a lack of sexual attraction to others, or low or absent interest in or desire for sexual activity. People who have similar experiences toward romantic relationships and actions are **aromantic**. Current statistics suggests that about 1 percent of the population is asexual, though many experts think the number may be higher.[122] River also uses the term **graysexual** to point toward their experiences of limited sexual attraction, where sex isn't entirely out of the picture, but it also isn't necessarily sought out.

So much of ace identity is defined by those who are non-ace as a *lack* of something. This kind of defining is exclusionary and diminishing, however, because for folks like River, ace

---

121 Megan Fletcher, "The Hypersexualization of the LGBTQ Community Is Still a Significant Issue," The Underground, September 1, 2016.
122 "10 Things You Need to Know about Asexuality," LGBTQ Life at Williams, May 1, 2020.

identity is just part of who they are. They aren't lacking anything. "The idea that asexual (and aromantic people) are lacking something makes it seem like there's something wrong with us, or that we aren't whole." This understanding is important when talking about asexuality, aromanticism, and even more identifiers recognizing the various levels and stages of romanticism and sexuality like **demi** identities (where romantic or sexual attraction depends on emotional connection). Someone can experience romantic desire without sexual feelings, and vice-versa.

Speaking with River was important for me and this book because I have found that the "A" found at the tail of "LGBTQIA+"—the abbreviated version of a much longer letter list—is often referred to by both people outside and inside the queer community as the "ally" letter. While allies are a vital part of both the past and future LGBTQ+ movements, I want to be better about not discounting ace identities, especially as we move forward.

As with many identities in this book, please be mindful that one person speaking about an identity is not the definitive statement about this word and experience. River was generous enough to share their experiences with me, and I am thrilled to be able to share these stories with you here. Just like how my sexuality can feel different than that of Robyn Ochs, for example, people identifying as both ace and nonbinary may feel differently to River. The reason for LGBTQ+ Revolution 2.0 is to prioritize the conversation—to open doors—over assumptions and hard lines.

River clarified, "I'm not repulsed by sexual attraction or sex at all, like some people who use 'ace' are. For me it's more like I have a very low libido. It's kind of in that gray area for me. If I were to have a partner in the future and they wanted to have sex, I think I would be fine with it, but it's not something that I prioritize." River has definitely had crushes, though, ones that have made them realize they were bi and pan-romantic.

They realized their romantic attraction to multiple genders before they understood their own gender identity and sexual preferences. Like many queer people, River's understandings did not come all at once but over time in an order of "Who do I like? What does this mean? Where do I fit? What actions do I want to take?" There aren't any roadmaps, but there are a variety of online communities free to access as long as you're willing to sift through conflicting information.

River, in fact, spent a lot of time in undergrad identifying as "**questioning**." They were asking questions of themself and of the socially constructed norms and terms around them and did not want to start using a word before feeling truly comfortable with it. This can be particularly blurry for folks attempting to address both their sexuality and their gender identity, amongst trying to just be eighteen and figure out a path in general. When River was asked to speak on LGBTQ+ panels, they would use questioning to help people understand that fluidity and exploration is a crucial element within understanding, and this term is not synonymous with inauthenticity.

"It's just a spectrum. And that can be confusing. It was very difficult because I could not easily conceptualize where I was outside of the opposite of sexual." And being defined in opposition to what is considered mainstream can be really ostracizing. Even on the online platforms River was able to find and use for their personal education, they found arguments over ace folks' place in the LGBTQ+ community. So many groups have all tried to find their own language to describe why they are both different than one another and similar in experiences to fall under the big queer umbrella. And how scary would it be to finally feel included in the queer world, only to see arguments break out over whether or not your identity makes the cut? To further "complicate" matters, plenty of people identify as hetero-romantic but asexual. They may not identify with the LGBTQ+ community in any way except that their sexual preferences are to not prioritize sexual engagement with their partners.

And if the big "We" of the LGBTQ+ community did not include ace folks, where would they find community? It's not a kink. It's not a club. Asexuality is a subset of the queer community, even if that can be hard for sexually minded people to understand.

Alongside cisgender hetero-romantic ace people, transgender ace and aro people have faced exclusionary treatment from others simply for liking people seen as the opposite presenting gender. These folks can be made to feel that they aren't valid because they were seen as "straight," even if they and their relationships were queer in nature. Some nonbinary people have also faced similar issues from people assuming their gender based off of their looks.

River also suspects that more women are publicly out as asexual versus men, obviously not because more women are asexual, but because of how differently men are raised in regards to pressures and expectations around sex and masculinity.

"I'll have conversations with my friends about this over and over. When you define romantic attraction, it can sound a lot like friendship. I know a number of queer people who kind of edge between friendship, platonic attraction, and romantic attraction. You may want to cuddle and hold hands, be close to someone, but draw a line at kissing. Your partner has to trust that you know yourself well enough that you know it's romantic and not simply friendship. It's definitely something—it feels different. If you experience both things, it's easier to know when they're separate." Talking about these various identities will hopefully help more people realize sooner that their experiences aren't weird or uncommon.

"I often thought my low libido and lack of interest in sex was actually something that was felt by most people and didn't realize that wasn't the case until college." River didn't have the terminology and language around asexuality that would have helped them understand this element of their relationships. This example and many more contribute to why I think ace identities need more representation in the LGBTQ+ community. Many of us could do a much better job communicating misunderstandings before jumping to inaccurate conclusions about what our partners, regardless of sexuality and gender, think and want.

Coming out for River was also a step-by-step process that still has not fully reached a conclusion. Admitting to developing crushes on any gender did not confuse their family too much, and they specifically received support on this end from their family. But they are only out as nonbinary and ace to their friends. They don't think their family would necessarily be upset, though—just confused. "I know it would be a conversation that would be difficult to have with my mother because it's hard to explain. Right now, I don't need to do that." The friends River made in undergrad helped them to know their questioning identity was valid, and they leaned on this chosen family to feel that unwavering love and support. Outside of this group, the pressure to back up both their nonbinary identity and asexuality can be exhausting.

"In a variety of areas of my life, my nonbinary identity might be handled differently. For the most part, I feel safe and accepted not just by my friends, but the LGBTQ+ community as a whole. However, even within LGBTQ+ circles, some people can be obsessed with binaries. Online, **transmedicalism** can be a thing. That's the belief that being transgender is linked to having gender dysphoria or transitioning. That kind of belief can be hard to see, especially if you're initially questioning your gender identity, and I know at times it's made me feel like my gender identity wasn't valid or like my gender was something I had to prove." This can translate into real-life fears quickly. When River started at their current company, they let people use she and her pronouns for the comfort of the coworkers. When River did decide they wanted to use their actual pronouns in the workplace, they were worried about causing a fuss.

"I realized that if you give someone the option of 'she and her,' and also 'they and them,' they will always default to the she and her unless they're some really practiced ally. I've gotten better at correcting people. When I realized I really was someone who needed they and them, I asked a warm, confident coworker to start using those pronouns for me—my pronouns—and to help correct people. He did that, and it took a lot of what I saw as a burden off of my own shoulders, which was really helpful and eased a lot of my discomfort."

Whether you've come across this book to celebrate queer identity, learn to be a better ally, or find narratives that help you to learn more about yourself, I think this story is particularly important to remember. So much of what you need to learn and experience will come with and from other LGBTQ+ people, but you can find people who do not have similar experiences who will still support you. Heck, often it's easier for them because while it does impact them, it isn't *about* them. This lesson in ally-ship is one I see constantly in my husband and one I value so much in many of my straight, cisgender friends. They hear me and value my perspective and want me to feel safe, without making themselves out to be some sort of hero on the front line. Basic tasks like correcting coworkers can be a hugely upsetting prospect for folks, and good allies will know how to assist without overstepping. It's all about openness and practice. This will help LGBTQ+ people focus on the more important aspects of community building.

River dreams of making queer spaces that are not sexualized and, while they won't exclude people who like to party, are more geared toward the LGBTQ+ personalities who aren't served as well by giant spectacles and large groups of people. "I don't drink. I just don't like the taste of alcohol and I'm generally not a party-scene person. Queer organizations are a big source for finding space, but sometimes I just want to watch anime or go to a bookstore or go to a museum… just hang out. It's getting easier, but I think we need more intentionally queer, intentionally chill places. Unfortunately, there aren't many spaces for queer introverts out in public." That's a large part of why more diverse queer narratives need to be told. River is hopeful they will see this change soon, and they are going to be putting efforts forward toward its creation.

XANY: COMING OUT IS ALMOST ALWAYS SCARY

Unfortunately, the process in coming capital O-U-T out is often terrifying, even when you are surrounded by supportive people. Xany Whitmoore (she/her) was about fifteen years old when she discovered she wasn't straight. If I had to bet, I'd say her discovery wasn't uncommon. She fell for her best friend.

"I already knew that my moms are together. I had queer role models in my life." Xany's parents are very active in the community, so she grew up going to barbecues with not only lesbians but also gender queer people, **polyamorous** (poly) people, and vocally kinky people.[123] Not all queer people are kinky—this is another layer of identification that some may be vocal about and some may not identify with, even in private. She had a lot of that open, broad exposure. As a teenager, she had access to language and queer acceptance at a time when a lot of people her age were only initially realizing what being gay meant.

Growing up with two moms, Xany already had an idea of how to examine these feelings she had about her friend, and she had the great benefit of knowing that the people around her would be supportive of her coming into her romantic and sexual identity, "The community around me basically said, 'Okay cool, let's roll with this,' and I know not everyone's journey is that simple."

The process itself was still nerve-racking, though. Xany set the scene for me while we were on the phone together, her normally strong and cheerful voice turning more purposeful and measured.

> "I was driving home with my mom one day and as we pulled into the neighborhood I said, 'I have to tell you something.' and she was like, 'Okay,' and I started crying. I said, 'I think I'm bi.' Her response was

---

[123] Ashley Mardell, *The ABC's of LGBT+*, (Mango Media Inc., 2016.), 12.

one of support and love and she said, 'Are you sure that's the word you want to use? Because a lot of people start there and it's okay if you need to change that word or if there's a different word.' So I said, 'No, that's the word.' And then she was crying and I was crying."

A puddle of mutual tears isn't exactly what most people would expect from a coming out story of a child to her lesbian mom, but I think Xany's story is important because it shows just how scary it still is to recognize and verbalize yourself as part of the LGBTQ+ community for the first time to loved ones, regardless of their positions within or outside of queerness.

So why is coming out so nerve-racking? Like any other fear, no series of sources is going to be exactly the same for anyone. We all grow up hearing different stories, witnessing a range of political events, and being surrounded by people with any number of views about sexuality and gender. Even for verbally supportive families of closeted children, it's one thing to support LGBTQ+ people in a more abstract, distant sense, but another thing when they'll have to support their own child.

In the interviews I held for this book, many of my peers stated they were nervous they would be letting their families down. That, even if their parents had never spoken negatively about LGBTQ+ people, there was a fear they would somehow be disappointed that their parental expectations hadn't been met. Coming out is difficult in these cases, despite past love and support, because there is often concern that the family will struggle to let go of whatever (likely heteronormative) vision they had in their minds for the life of their child.

Crying can be a part of many coming out stories, as Xany experienced. Tears can happen for many reasons, including feelings of relief and sobriety. Sobriety because she likely knew all too well the struggles that come with identifying as an LGBTQ+ person in America, even with the rewards found in the community's resilience and luminance. The ease of a child's life is often a case made by parents for why they initially wished their kid was straight. Until society changes, admitting to the potential roadblocks that come from telling the truth makes coming out feel startlingly real.

When Xany came out she was saying, "This is who I am, this is who I want to be, and this is how I want you to both accept and see me." The words, "I think I might be bi," and the uncertainty suggested did not take away the declaration that she was finding herself in the LGBTQ+ community and that she felt she belonged within it. Speaking her mind made her sexuality true, something she would have a difficult time denying if she found herself wanting to do so. She was showing who she really was and that vulnerability, even to one of the people who loves her most, was scary.

Coming out can also be scary because, for anyone who sees themselves as part of the LGBTQ+ community or at least in the vicinity of being part of it, realizing both sexual orientation or gender identity and sharing that information with family and friends isn't usually a clear-cut process. More often than not, coming out is a gradual process that has to slowly unfold over multiple years. We often have to do it over and over again, both to ourselves, our loved ones, and to new people in our lives.

According to a survey conducted by Pew Research Center in 2013 of LGBTQ+ Americans, **86 percent reported that they had told one or more close friends about their sexual orientation or gender identity. More impressive, 54 percent said that all or most of the important people in their life knew that they were lesbian, gay, bisexual, or transgender.**[124]

The Pew study found large differences here across LGB groups. Lesbians and gay men were more likely than bisexual individuals to have told at least one close friend about their sexual orientation (96 percent of gay men and 94 percent of lesbians, compared with only 79 percent of bisexuals). The first two groups are also much more likely to report that most of the people who are important to them are aware of their sexual orientation: 77 percent of gay men and 71 percent of lesbians say all or most people know, compared with only 28 percent of bisexuals.[125]

Among bisexuals, there are large gender differences between those who state that the people closest to them know that they are bisexual. Roughly 88 percent of bisexual women said they had told a close friend about their sexual orientation, while only

---

124 Pew Research Center, "Chapter 3: The Coming Out Experience." *Pew Research Center's Social & Demographic Trends Project*, December 31, 2019.
125 Pew Research Center, 2019.

55 percent of bisexual men said they had done the same. Similarly, while one out of three of bisexual women said that most of the important people in their lives knew about their bisexuality, only 12 percent of bisexual men reported this information.[126]

Additionally, a whopping 65 percent of bisexual men stated that only a few or none of the important people in their lives knew they are bisexual.[127] Why? Mark Lees at the Bisexual Resource Center wrote this is likely because out of those in the LGBTQ+ community, bisexual men have been the least portrayed in television and movies.[128] Expectations around masculinity create masks on bisexual men that are difficult to remove—they often grow up without examples of well-known men who are bisexual and are still *perceived* as masculine.[129] Like bisexuals of different genders, bisexual men have concerns around complicating their relationships with their family and other support systems.[130] Expectations around masculinity seep into the minds of women as well, and much in a similarly damaging way that men hyper-sexualize bisexual women, women de-sexualize bisexual men—refusing to believe they can be attracted to men without being solely gay.[131] As more bisexual men, like Vishaal Reddy from our media chapter, come out and stand as examples of men with joyful lives, societal acceptance and validation of them will gradually become the norm.[132] Much

---

126 Pew Research Center, 2019.
127 Pew Research Center, 2019.
128 Mark Lees, "Coming Out as a Bisexual Man: The 5 Reasons Why We Don't," Bisexual Resource Center, November 6, 2019.
129 Lees, 2019.
130 Lees, 2019.
131 Lees, 2019.
132 Lees, 2019.

of this change, this acceptance of bi and pansexual people of all genders and romantic preferences, has to come from the more heavily represented queer identities and our allies. Consistent, real-life examples can make a world of difference to a young person coming out, but it does not mean that conversation isn't still intimidating.

Growing up around gay people also didn't mean that Xany immediately knew everything. She started building additional vocabulary after finding online forums for young people under eighteen years of age. This is where she learned about pansexuality and queerness as umbrella terms. Neither of these connected with her soul quite the same way bisexual did at the time, but gathering words like collector's items allowed her to check and recheck the accuracy of the terminology she was using in reference to herself.

I met Xany my first year in undergrad. Her openness around her sexuality contributed to my own willingness to be out. As I mentioned earlier, I did not feel gay enough to join the queer organizations in college. This was a self-restriction I wish I hadn't weighed upon myself with the rest of the ridiculousness that was undergrad, but Xany makes me feel like I could come out individually to people over and over again, and that made a huge difference to my self-confidence and self-acceptance. I cannot imagine how much more difficult this would have been for both of us if we were affected by toxic expectations around masculinity. We will continue to push for representation, acceptance, and celebration so that coming out might get a little less scary for future generations, like LGBTQ+ people have done before us.

ARI:
ONLINE COMMUNITY

—

Ari Drennen (she/her) could not begin to figure out her gender identity until she stepped back and recognized that the rules we have around gender are arbitrary. Meaningless. While the way she exists within those rules is important to her in order to feel safe, she needed to understand that, truly, she did not need to fit perfectly into some predetermined narrative.

Especially for **transgender** (anyone whose gender does not match the sex or gender they were assigned at birth) people like Ari, there can be a pressure to say "I knew I was _____ from a young age."[133] But sometimes that isn't accurate. Old memories can be warped, forgotten, or need to be rethought in order for those "early signs" to emerge from the depths of the mind. It's perfectly normal not to have a long list of examples of why an assigned gender was incorrect. Ari told me, "What is important is to be able to take steps to make yourself more comfortable with who you are without waiting to have the picture 100 percent formed."

Early in Ari's transition, seeing other people who had a somewhat binary presentation but who identified as nonbinary was really important to her. She didn't feel comfortable claiming a female identity at that point in her transition, but there was a YouTube series, *The Wondrous Life of Caleb Gallo*, with a character called Freckle who had feminine pronouns but also had stubble and wasn't on hormones. This character existed in a space where gender wasn't important. Ari watched that whole series twice in a row. Platforms without a paywall and with ease of access for creators like YouTube are great for finding LGBTQ+ information and community.

Ari was able, with this example and others, to embrace that her gender did not need to meet a list of requirements to be valid. She saw Sarah McBride, the first trans woman to speak at a Democratic National Convention, and was completely moved. Ari had just started a job on Hillary Clinton's

---

133 Mardell, Ashley, "The ABC's of LGBT+," (Mango Media Inc., 2016), 14.

presidential campaign, "and I was really scared about the idea that I could be who I was and still be involved in political conversations and might not be taken seriously. Seeing Sarah McBride on that stage was so important."

Donald Trump winning the presidential election in 2016, though, felt like a huge setback. It led Ari to question if the United States had progressed as she thought it had.

"But then, in 2017, when Danica Roem was the first transgender lawmaker to win a state house seat in Virginia, I regained so much hope."

When Roem won, Ari watched intently, searing the images on the television into her memory. When her partner came home, Ari was sobbing on the bed, "because watching her helped me to know that *I* could do it." So, she stopped getting haircuts and started to dive deep into what kind of person she actually wanted to be.

The dive wasn't wholly positive, however. She found so much information on the trans-related pages on Reddit, but quickly realized those spaces could sometimes be negative. "They're certainly helpful for people sharing their experiences and answering some nuts-and-bolts questions, but there are a lot of cruel people and unhelpful comparisons on those pages."

Twitter ended up serving Ari better. It became a space for her to easily meet other people and connect over hashtags and private messages. "There is an image of Twitter as a hotbed for hate. But, as someone with a medium number of followers, I haven't found too much harassment and have been able to meet a lot of other people with whom I went on to form real-world friendships." And these connections were genuine, whether or not Ari ever ended up meeting these people offline.

Ari had never known another trans person prior to these internet explorations. Though Ari didn't always avail herself of this option, Twitter is a place where people often create "alternate" Twitter accounts. Many people exploring both gender and sexuality will practice their identities through these other personas before coming out in the real world. While this is something to keep in mind with any relationship or friendship formed online, these opportunities are crucial for people who need feedback in order to build confidence in their "new" social interactions.

"I never created an alternate account, but I know other people do this to explore their gender identity before they're out to friends and family. Part of me wished I had done that because I honestly felt so alone at the beginning." Ideas around catfishing (lying about who you are online) popped into my head during this conversation. We are constantly taught to be wary of inaccurate profiles online. This, however, is different. Online spaces have served as opportunities for people to *finally* experience being themselves, and this does not hurt anyone in the way that catfishing does.

Not all platforms are created equal for trans people coming out as themselves, however. "Instagram can be tough because it's so curated and so Photoshopped. I remember really early in my transition looking at trans women on Instagram and thinking, 'Oh my god, these are perfect humans… I could never.' Twitter is just a little easier because it's not as image-focused." Like anything else, preferences for platforms are different, even within the trans community.

In 2019, 24 percent of Americans reported having a close friend or family member who is transgender. That's more than double the 11 percent who reported knowing a trans person in 2011.[134]

While unproven to be directly related, I think the rise of YouTube and Tumblr allowed trans people to become content creators on their own, making honest content that surpassed the way cisgender people previously perceived them. I remember getting the bulk of my LGBTQ+ education through these platforms and learning how to be a better ally to the trans and nonbinary communities by reading post after post. I am definitely still learning as well, and these free platforms provide confidence that the right knowledge is out there if I can make the time to wade through some misinformation.

Nick Adams, director of transgender representation at the LGBTQ+ media advocacy organization GLAAD, told Vox that trans young people have been "able to go onto YouTube and develop these really strong relationships with trans content creators who talk about their transitions because they're interactive in a way that mainstream media is not."[135]

---

134 Daniel Greenberg, "America's Growing Support for Transgender Rights," PRRI, accessed May 1, 2020.
135 Katelyn Burns, "The Internet Made Trans People Visible. It Also Left Them More Vulnerable," Vox, December 27, 2019.

Ari and I briefly discussed Natalie Wynn's YouTube channel, ContraPoints. Wynn announced her transition on her YouTube channel, opening up a previously text-based educational experience to a more substantial, audio-visual one. Other YouTubers like Kat Blaque, a Black trans woman, speak to both trans issues and an assortment of content, helping viewers solidify the knowledge that trans folks, like everyone else, have multifaceted interests, identities, and aspirations.[136]

Twitter, Reddit, and other internet forums helped to ease some of Ari's anxieties around transitioning, physically and even mentally and emotionally. She went in slowly, carefully reflecting on how posting made her feel and allowing those positive reinforcements to seep into her real life as well.

Like coming out online, Ari's offline coming out journey was not a singular, large announcement, but a gradual process with each individual in her life. "I had a lot of trouble with my parents when I first came out. My mom's one of those people who originally said, 'You don't need to be trans because gender norms shouldn't exist.'"

Ari's mother's understanding of the damage often caused by gender expectations initially prevented her from accepting her child, and the two are still working toward healing and empathizing with one another. Her feminism came from a place where makeup, for example, is a tool of the patriarchy. "So, when I wore makeup, she viewed that as my participation in that oppression. She thinks of my femininity as

---

136 Sandra Song, "Kat Blaque Doesn't Give a Fuck," PAPER, September 11, 2019.

problematic, but she doesn't realize that it was an important part of my transition." These conflicts are not without glimmers of light, however.

Over Christmas in 2019, Ari's mother gave her a beautiful silver snowflake necklace, a nod to Ari's passion for ice skating. "That was really meaningful because it was like she saw *me*. Now, I wear it almost all the time."

And Ari is really good about identifying moments like these that help her to recognize happiness within herself. In fact, registering her own emotions has become increasingly easier as her body and mind have received the hormones they needed. "Once I started hormones, every single thing in my life became easier. People focus on the physical changes so much, but when I had the right hormones in my body, everything got better."

Ari had been terrified of jumping into taking hormones, but the beneficial mental health impacts came so quickly for her that she now feels that her current personality is the one she'd been hoping to have her entire life. "It was a genuinely effective treatment for gender dysphoria for me. And it made my life so much easier. With dysphoria, a lot of times you can't really realize how it's affecting you every day until it's gone. So much of my personality before had really been a series of coping mechanisms. I was so introverted before."

Before hormones, Ari felt joy and self-expression in painting her nails and shaving her legs. While she still enjoys these things, she no longer needs to do them to mitigate her dysphoria.

> "I could be running around the woods filthy, like I haven't shaved in a week, and I would still feel like myself now in a way I never was able to before."

Transitioning, coming out, and any other steps in these processes are a journey that will likely look and feel different for every individual. It is vital to remember that it is a *journey* that will not be simple and that will take reflection, check-ins, acknowledgments, and hard work. "It's not like you're flipping a switch," said Ari. "I know people who figure out their gender identity as they figure out their sexual identity. I know others who have tried on a bunch of different labels and that's okay. It's okay to not get it 100 percent right the first time. If all you know is you're not cis or you're not straight, that is a more than fine place to start."

It is crucial to feel at home in your body and brain. "I don't look in the mirror and see an unrealistic image of myself. I look in the mirror and see what other people see. Often people who are anti-trans will compare being trans to having body dysmorphia, and they'll say that you don't treat dysmorphia by indulging people but by telling them that they're wrong about what they look like. This is different. This is dysphoria." Misunderstandings like these often prevent cisgender people, even within the LGBTQ+ community, from understanding the particular needs and challenges faced by trans people. As allies, we need to do more than simply follow trans people on social media and serve as internet-warriors for them (though, in some cases, this is helpful). Allies need to hire trans people. Listen to trans people. Hang out with trans people. With passion and determination in her voice, Ari told me simply, "We just need the room to succeed and be supported and loved." Let's make that room.

ALEXIS: GIFTING BOUNDARIES

Alexis Moore (she/her) started to figure that she was queer toward the end of college. She grew up in a pretty strict Christian household and struggled with phases of seeking sanctuary in Christianity, then abandoning it, then finding a more comfortable relationship with it, and continuing this cycle. "I found myself in a more atheist mindset, and so I've always had this flip flop between my politics that I believe and the religion that I can relate to." Alexis identifies as "atheist-ish" and has learned to create her own space and community outside of religious spaces.

After Alexis allowed herself to really read and learn more about what it meant to be pansexual, her mindset opened up. "I knew I wasn't into the physical as much. I think people are beautiful, regardless of their gender and how they present. But because my parents were always talking about grandkids, sexuality was heteronormative in my household."

This led Alexis to present as a straight woman early on, both to others and to herself. "I don't think they would understand. So I never really came out. I remember wearing shirts with 'LGBT fine by me' written on them for a school event and my parents sat me down to say that wearing that, promoting that, wasn't okay."

In this conversation, Alexis respectfully fought back. She stated directly that she understood what the shirt was saying and that she believed her parents' disapproval was wrong. This was never really resolved between the family, and Alexis cites these moments of extreme homophobia within her household as a huge source of tension and inner turmoil she still contends with today.

"After graduating college, I joined a nonprofit spiritual community that was mostly Christian in Denver. The pastor was a strong, liberal woman who helped me realize that forcing myself to go to church because of the group I was a part of seemed more harmful than helpful to me."

Allowing herself to feel her worries, rather than suppressing them, helped her to figure out where she needed to go and who she wanted in her life. She was in a Christian program but soon found herself desiring to be in a place where questions were encouraged, not muffled. "I told them I didn't want to pray with them. Because I didn't believe in God. And they told me I had to leave." Alexis couldn't change her truth to stay in her community, and she shouldn't have needed to abandon a community that had promised her welcoming safety. The group had upheld negative Christian values, prioritizing image over individual.

The experience of leaving this community but developing positive relationships with others in Denver was liberating for Alexis, and even her roommates were helpful in her exploration of her Blackness, her womanhood, and her queerness. "For all of us to be alike but ourselves, in both sexuality and religion, or spirituality… all these things can flow together. I found the right people, and it was amazing."

Alexis had made a point to embrace the moments where she thought, "Oh, that makes sense." These moments happened with people, when she was alone, and even when she was thinking about completely unrelated problems and topics. Small, peaceful breaths would surprise her, and she made a point to notice.

Tension between people who are and are not involved in religion and spirituality is a tricky subject for me. I went to Catholic school while growing up, and my gut response to these conversations is that religion is a socially constructed and an unnecessary stressor—something that only gives folks excuses to discriminate against LGBTQ+ people. This kind of mentality has proven to be useless over and over again in my life, though, and breaking my own bias toward religious people is something I am still tackling within myself. I have to acknowledge how ingrained some homophobic ideas are within some churches and faiths and that many of the people who believe them do so because they think of it as the Word of God, not as a manmade prejudice. Plenty of nondenominational religious spaces have rejected homophobia in favor of teachings that promote true peace for everyone. Luckily, Alexis found solace in her own built communities and those she found online.

> "People were really helpful. They were people of color who were also queer, and they helped me fall into it and feel a safety net. They showed me what was possible and how powerful being Black and queer and a woman can be."

Alexis had found space.

She has recently moved to California and will be seeking a similar, queer-and-of-color community. She has surrounded herself there with people who do not identify as LGBTQ+ but are great allies. They do not bat an eye when she talks about her queerness, and their questions are never probing or overtly sexual. She doesn't feel the need to prove herself to them because of the confidence she has built within herself over time. I admire Alexis's self-work so much because she invested that time and understanding into her goals for self-love and acceptance. She balances leaning on others and relying on herself beautifully.

Part of Alexis's adventure to California stemmed from a new partner, someone she met while exploring what it was that she wanted from her romantic partnerships in Denver. "I started dating him at around the same time I was dating five other people. I was trying out open relationships and understanding what all those things meant to me." This partner, Adam, stuck and is providing a huge element of comfort and joy in Alexis's life. This journey had roadblocks and storms, but within it, Alexis found the way that she loved to love and be loved. "I feel like myself."

Alexis's journey has definitely been one of hardship and constant self-assurance and reflection. Her story depicts some of the tough parts of figuring out the boundaries of identity. Oftentimes, it can be really hard to understand what sexuality is and how important or unimportant it can be to somebody, especially because these things can often shift in multiple directions.

"One weekend, when I went home to Memphis, I was thinking about coming out to my family. And then, I don't remember the exact conversation, but my parents shamed someone for being gay." This is painful. I have had people make homophobic comments in front of me and have not always had the energy to fight them on these views while also being careful enough not to damage the relationship. Sometimes remaining quiet seems like the best option, even when it hurts.

After the hateful remarks, Alexis went up to her room and immediately drew an image of her internal feelings, her heart broken after having been so hopeful about the idea of finally being able to fully be herself with her family. But she was not able to feel safe in that environment, and that was devastating.

She described the drawing to me, scribbled in her notebook—a ball that mirrored the way she herself had curled upon her bed. It shook me, realizing that the people who raised Alexis had unknowingly sent her out of their space. She did not just need to escape them physically in that moment but needed to stay away in order to handpick the people with whom she could feel safe.

Instead of completely removing herself from her family, a group of people she loves so dearly, she is gifting them with her own boundaries. Alexis can now confidently speak to them about LGBTQ+ issues and is taking her time in deciding how much of her own experience to share. "I do a little bit of conceptual work with them. I speak up about homophobic and transphobic incidents, but I do not allow them the space to know that their comments and actions also apply to and harm me. It is currently the safest way I know to support myself in those hard spaces."

Part of boundary-setting and people-finding is knowing what you need and from where you can receive these needs. While Alexis's family is not LGBTQ+ affirming, they provide a space for her to enjoy and learn about her Trinidadian culture. Removing herself from this opportunity in favor of LGBTQ+ spaces would likely make her feel safe in her sexuality but significantly underrepresented in her culture. "My family affirms my culture and ethnicity so wholly, and when I am with non-Black or non-Trinidadian friends, I don't receive that same type of love." No particular culture, space, religion, group, or even individual is inherently safe or inherently harmful. Alexis has learned that gifting herself with boundaries and appreciating the different kinds of love and support she can receive from the people in her life is most important.

TRISHA:
IT CAN BE SMALL

Trisha Gupta (she/her), an Indian woodblock artist and immigration activist, discovered she wasn't straight when she was in college. The relationship she developed with another woman wasn't necessarily sexual, but it was definitely romantic.

She had always admired women, and had only really considered personality when examining her attraction to other people. After surviving a sexual assault, Trisha became very turned off by drinking culture and the dynamic of gendered power that the men around her seemed to feel in party spaces. She described to me that once she even had a drink poured on her after politely turning a man down for a dance.

After these experiences, Trisha was unable to un-see structural gender dynamics and the gender-performances put on by the people around her. She realized how many gender conventions of the way that women are "supposed" to operate were coming out at her detriment. The women around her were playing into roles that they felt they were supposed to play into because of how relationships and gender are discussed in wider society.

We discussed Trisha's upbringing in a community very influenced by Indian culture and the ways that gender dynamics are both dissimilar and exactly the same in India and the United States. "We have arranged marriage, but the conventions that occur in Western society are as damaging and unavoidable. A taught dynamic can occur between women with power and unnecessary jealousy, often linked to sexuality." In my own observations I have witnessed how the encouragement of competition between women is something we still have to actively push against.

In fact, what looks like hostile competition between women does not come across the same way when the same actions are taken by men. Men are typically raised to be comfortable with competition, viewing winning as essential. When women feel the same way, they are labeled as insecure. This societal pressure can make it uncomfortable for a woman to share and enjoy her accomplishments with friends, particularly other women, which ends up hurting people like Trisha, who consequently avoid friendships with people of really any gender for fear of experiencing drama.[137]

"I did receive some really important support after my assault. A group of women put pink balloons and streamers on my dorm room door multiple days after it happened, and that was very sweet. A man also offered to hang out while I slept the first couple of nights after it happened too—just chill out in the same room, so I would feel safe."

These individuals and the presence of a particularly empowering friend were vital for Trisha to remember how wonderful friendships truly were—something that happens to many young women. When bullies and genuine insecurities last into college and sometimes even later, it can be difficult not to say, "I'm not like other women." Statements like this only cause women to internalize misogyny, preventing beneficial collaborations and relationship formations. I am thrilled at the woman-power, feminist movement, and the ways in which current young generations do not seem to view "cattiness" as the norm for women. Trisha was not lucky enough to experience mostly positive relationships with women throughout her teens, but one friend was able to change her own biases.

Trisha met a young woman who changed her outlook. "She was pretty much exactly the kind of person I wanted to be like. She had two cats. She saw me free from all of the stereotypes norms that were put on both of us."

---

137 Lynn Margolies, "Competition among Women: Myth and Reality," Psych Central, October 8, 2018.

Nia* pushed Trisha to be more artistic. She was a pole-dancer and used this talent to raise money for survivors of sexual assault. Through her, Trisha found a big, majority-queer community of women who had a version of her life experience, all, in Trisha's words, "Confident, and therefore hot as hell." Nia did not view herself as in competition with other women but as an advocate for them.

Trisha herself is a great dancer but hates going to clubs because she values personal space. After meeting Nia, she went to a pole dancing event where the women were acknowledging their sexuality, the power of their own bodies, and the art form's athleticism without being objectified. This loosened Trisha's views about hating clubs, and she allowed Nia to start taking her to gay clubs.

"There was this green area with darts in the back. You could talk, and honestly, no woman ever approached me in a solely sexual manner. They would come over and ask politely, "Hey, can we dance?" It was thrilling for Trisha to have those short conversations without fear of backlash. Men in her past had reacted negatively to being turned down, but she did not have to fear this response at these queer clubs. "I remember the first time I ever hit on a woman myself. It felt a little like a betrayal toward Nia. We weren't in a relationship, but that was when I really registered my feelings."

Trisha and Nia had an intense relationship. She told me that sometimes, when spending time together, they would fall asleep beside each other and, without any sort of physical contact, there seemed to be an almost partner-like dynamic. Trisha would just show up at Nia's home with flowers when she was feeling down sometimes. The line between friendship and partnership for these two was fairly thin and confusing, and it eventually put enough of a strain on the pair that it was hard to ignore.

Trisha decided that even though she held love and respect for Nia, she wanted to find another, confirmed, relationship. This decision brought back pressures from the outside world like an unceasing wave.

> "I felt this need to try and have a boyfriend to look straight and be straight."

We talked about how this doesn't quite work out that way—choosing a male partner did not diminish Trisha's queerness. She didn't have anything to prove, and she picked a partner, not a side. The pressures she felt do matter, though, and she looks on her experiences with women with fondness and reflects on her experiences when she can, so as not to lose touch with this part of herself.

The woman Trisha hit on at the club ended up dating Nia. The LGBTQ+ dating worlds in most cities are hilariously and tragically small. Gay Twitter is full of disheartening jokes about how small queer circles tend to be. But to Trisha's surprise, "It was totally fine with me because I think they got along better anyway. I love that I felt free in the fact that Nia approached that woman afterward. I admired that they both knew I was queer without me needing to state it because I didn't know what to do with it, but they were willing to work with me." Even in circumstances that could have been messy, Trisha's friends prioritized her well-being over pressuring her to label herself and stick to some prescribed way of dating.

These relationships allowed Trisha to explore what she thought about gender and relationships, releasing her from the strictness put upon her by others. "So, they kind of changed my life. They really brought me into this world where I had a safe place. That experience helped me have a relationship that felt right to me later because I learned to trust and see people as people. And I approached my husband that way. I would never have been able to do that if Nia hadn't been a part of my life."

The two still speak sometimes. Nia also married a man and has continued working to empower black LGBTQ+ women.

In many ways, gender expectations are defied by those in the LGBTQ+ community. While some folks do find sparks of joy in social expectations because it can take pressure off of some decisions, people with Trisha's experiences often feel more in control and empowered by seeing themselves outside of these limiting structures.

Trisha found safety and someone who recognized her queerness in a single friendship. One person invited her into a community that changed her outlook on friendships and her place in the world. Giving power to others can be that simple. It can be that small.

VALERIE: FINDING VOCABULARY

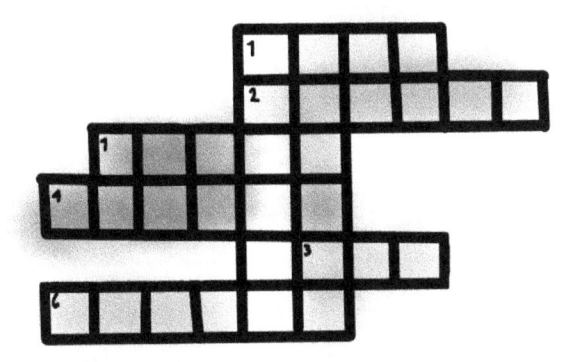

Valerie Novack (she/her) primarily identifies herself as queer. But, like anything, that shifts. Something that is not necessarily particular to the LGBTQ+ community but still prominent is language use. It's there in the title: LGBTTQQIAAP (Lesbian, Gay, Bisexual, Transgender, Transsexual, Queer, Questioning, Intersex, Asexual, Ally,

Pansexual).[138] A number of variants recognize communities claiming these letters, and the list is much longer and always evolving with some words becoming obsolete and new ones becoming prominent. People with disabilities, for example, often see themselves as part of that larger group, and then their disability and the categorization that comes with that helps them locate smaller communities. In the queer community, we name ourselves. This can get tricky when context, safety, and time all come into the conversation.

Valerie identifies with both the queer community and the disability community. She walked me through her current vocabulary and the path she took to discover and rediscover her favorite titles. "For someone like me, it is very much a choice because so many things about me are not immediately visible." Valerie cites this lack of immediate visibility as the reason she has become so vocal. "I am biracial and often look 'ethnically ambiguous.' I remember all through school, there was no 'more than one race' option on scantron sheets."

In middle school, she stopped choosing her race on forms like these because she often either had to pick Hispanic or Black. Often, the Black option specifically said "not Hispanic" in parenthesis, which blatantly excluded her identity. "I didn't know then that this whole idea of 'picking a side' was going to be the theme of my life, and that my refusal to do that, even at eleven and twelve would be indicative of my overall nature."

---

138 "Family Services of Peel." Family Services of Peel, April 12, 2019.

Valerie also married a man who has fibromyalgia and dysautonomia (POTs), as well as major depression and a personality disorder. "I have a less visible disability. So, many times I can 'pass' as non-disabled as well. Instead, part of how I make my living is by making sure people know I am disabled, even if I don't 'look' it." She is married and polyamorous, so her wedding ring leads many people to have assumptions that she only sleeps with her partner.

Some of this vocabulary and identity balancing can be hard to maneuver. "Even within the disability community, I often find myself being put in situations where I am asked to prioritize my disabled-ness over my Blackness, womanhood, or queerness." Valerie made a vow to herself that she wouldn't let these struggles overcome her after a failed suicide attempt put her in the ICU for several days and the psych ward for longer.

> "I promised myself if I had to be on this Earth, I was no longer going to allow my identities to be split between groups because I am a *whole* Black, Mexican, queer, poly, disabled, married slut, and either you are okay with that or you aren't."

Like many other people in the LGBTQ+ community, Valerie sometimes uses the context of conversation to steer her identifying information, "I might, if somebody were to ask me my sexual orientation for some reason, be more specific in some situations. I may say, 'Well, I'm pansexual.' But when I say that, I'm really only talking about what kind of person I am attracted to, not what kind of person I am. So, I find queer more of an accurate descriptor to explain my whole being." The signs we use only tell us so much.

This multi-layer, intersectional identity encompassed at least in part by "queer" is important to describe because one can be part of the LGBTQ+ community and not necessarily be sexually active. On the other hand, they can also be romantically attracted to some people but physically attracted to others. Not everything lines up in a predictable way for everyone. So, while Valerie uses "pansexual" to mean that her attraction is not enhanced or hindered by someone's gender presentation, the nonsexual aspect of the community to which she relates is not explained by her pan-ness.

When asked about her journey to the term "queer," Valerie explained, "When I was younger, I identified as bisexual. I don't even know if I heard the term pansexual. But, at the time, 'bisexual' had that binary associated with it." Pansexual seems less restrictive to many people, and for Valerie this word seemed more appropriate. Lately, identifying as bisexual has not been used to assert the binary (just man versus woman), but Valerie didn't want to constantly have to extend the conversation unnecessarily. The term pansexual was a fairly clear way to describe herself to others.

People seem to understand pan as meaning that attraction can come regardless of a person's gender. "That suited me. Then, 'queer' started to sit with me more when I started to register how much happier using that term made me feel. I found myself in **polyamorous** (poly) communities, for example, that speak to my sexuality but aren't orientation-based." Around the same time, Valerie started realizing new things about herself and what she wanted from her relationships. "I started identifying as queer because it spoke to both my sexual orientation and my style of love and romanticism."

Valerie is in what is sometimes called a "straight-presenting marriage," where the assumption is that because a couple looks like a heterosexual, cisgender pair, they aren't part of the LGBTQ+ community. She did assume she would be in a relationship like this (straight-appearing) growing up because of the context in which she was raised, but this did not keep her from recognizing the ways both her identity and the vocabulary she used around it changed over time.

"The first crush I remember having was on a woman. If I had been in a household that had been more supportive of me exploring those feelings, I might not have realized I liked guys as well."

For Valerie, there was never a question of whether or not she liked women. Every kind of introductory sexual moment she could recall for me had happened with a woman. "But I had no doubt in my mind I would grow up and marry a man and I was going have kids because that was God's plan." Eliminating an attraction to men was out of the question. Marriage was for her like it is for many young women—an assumption thrust upon her by her family and peers.

What some people may view as a sad story, however, has a bit of humor to it. There was a lightness in Valerie's voice as she told me these things. She doesn't regret partnering with a man. On the contrary, "I think I probably would have identified as lesbian first, and then I would have met some men when I was older who would have made me realize I like men as well." This is a completely topsy-turvy version of the "regular" queer narrative, where a person initially recognizes attraction to someone of a different gender and does not realize until later that they are actually queer. All our paths are different.

I haven't had the opportunity to meet anyone who needed to re-come out as more fluid than gay, but I have heard of this happening. This unhelpfully gets picked up by some conservatives as proof that being gay is a choice, but the existence of this hateful idea does not mean people like Valerie should feel they *have* to partner with anyone in particular. This fluidity and openness is, in large part, the reason why bi and pansexual people like Valerie and me get left out and self-exclude ourselves from gay communities; their privilege of being able to choose a heteronormative (though this labeling is hugely arguable) presentation makes them a target at which the haters and internal insecurities can aim.

Being ourselves, though, is most important. Without heavy Christian influences, Valerie probably would have started off identifying as a lesbian person first and a pansexual person later. It's difficult to come out on many levels, but it was difficult for us to imagine what it would have taken to "backtrack" a bit after the realization that gender was not what defined our attractions. What would re-coming out look like then?

Valerie has not allowed external assumptions of her partnership to prevent her from finding a queer community to call home. Nobody should let fears about how other people might label them prevent them from seeking the fuel they need to feel assured in themselves and find people who celebrate them. I realize this is more easily said than done, but community creation is important and should not be overlooked because of confusion around vocabulary or outside pressures.

"Maybe some kind of subconscious thing brings us (queer people) together. I actually, in just the last couple of years, have been absolutely finding ways to be verbal about that and about who I think I am. A big part of that is because I *crave* community. I know I want to be seen."

In a study that pulled data from an LGBTQ+ National Teen Study developed in collaboration with the Human Rights Campaign, seventeen thousand teens were surveyed, coming from a range of race, ethnicity, and socioeconomic statuses. Twenty-six percent of these teenagers chose emerging sexual identity labels over traditional labels.[139]

More recently, efforts have been made in academic research to request LGBTQ+ identification from youth in order to best represent this population. Problematically, however, most researchers are familiar with labels like lesbian, gay, and bisexual, but are less privy to "new" terms ("new" is quoted because a term being used in broader circulation does not

---

[139] "Many LGBTQ Youth Don't Identify with Traditional Sexual Identity Labels." EurekAlert! February 13, 2019.

necessarily make the word novel). Still, many people tasked with sociological research ignore even the traditional identifiers. The 2020 United States Census included questions about household relationships for the first time, but the nature of the questions limited the representation of single LGBTQ+ individuals.[140]

Thousands of people make up the LGBTQ+ population but are not being counted when resources are considered. Even if these important inquiries were in the census, it would not be enough to simply ask about these traditional labels—lesbian, gay, bisexual. There are too many variables, and identities are often fluid and layered.

Just in the LGBTQ+ National Teen Study, thousands of teenagers most commonly use new identity labels that researchers have not yet heard. Ryan J. Watson, who led the study, stated, "This is vexing, given there are likely hundreds of thousands of youth who are using terms like pansexual and nonbinary. It's important for researchers especially to capture what the nuanced experiences might be of these youth. We don't want to miss them. We want to make sure we capture what these youth want to be called; the identities they actually are identifying with. We think that's pretty important."[141]

If researchers don't know that the lesser-known communities within the larger LGBTQ+ umbrella exist, these groups are not fought for or understood by academic advocates. The

---

140 Hansi Wang, "2020 Census Will Ask About Same-Sex Relationships," *NPR*, March 30, 2018.
141 "Many LGBTQ Youth Don't Identify with Traditional Sexual Identity Labels." EurekAlert! February 13, 2019.

diversity in the LGBTQ+ community necessitates broader descriptors around gender and sexuality on national surveys. Watson proposed a write-in option. This is important for the same reasons that led Valerie to wish to update her own vocabulary. Pansexual people have different experiences, some privileges and some obstacles, than gay people. All of this becomes even more important when we begin to layer in gender, race, socioeconomic standing, and more identifiers. Asking these questions matters to LGBTQ+ health and livelihood. The numbers of young people and adults coming out as fluid or solid within various LGBTQ+ identities mean we must be flexible to new terminology. We need to ask, to be open to what our teens' sexual and gender identities are, and to be vocal ourselves.

In addition to this, we must work to make the LGBTQ+ community more inclusive overall and not assume we can understand someone's racial identity, disability status, mental health, or anything about them, really, solely based on our siloed, often visual contexts.

HAFSA: IDENTITY IN MULTITUDES

Hafsa Qureshi (she/her), Stonewall's 2019 Bi Role Model of the Year and LGBTQ+ Muslim woman, has dealt with both hyper-sexualization and apathy around her layers of identity. When she tells people she is bisexual, she is often met with the assumption she is sexually active. Not only this, but people will also suspect she has multiple partners and this was a "lifestyle" she chose out of selfishness, not a truth she discovered about her identity. "But some people choose not to be in an intimate relationship. When you come out, people want to ask you about sex, but that's very private and personal."[142]

This phenomenon is odd and, while it isn't unique to the LGBTQ+ community, it is so thoroughly spoken of within the bi, pan, and queer community that I have run into the issue at least one hundred times throughout my research. Personally, I have to dance around the topic of sex with every person I come out to—especially after getting married. I don't ask my cisgender straight friends how they discovered they preferred their partner's gender or about their general sexual habits, but I have needed to find a multitude of ways to prove my sexuality without detailing my past. I should add that I have not been successful in this search. I've mostly become fluent in the conversation-swerve.

Hafsa Qureshi combats this same problem with added complications due to societal expectations around her religion. Her hijab signals to people carrying both unintentional and intentional biases about Muslim folks that she couldn't possibly be both religious and queer, so she isn't queer. She can't be. This ridiculous assumption stems from the same structural oddities that prevent people raised in religion, like me, from knowing how exactly to communicate that one identity does not discredit the other. Hafsa's visual signal of her faith garners more scrutiny from people who do not understand multiplicity or who do not care to view her as, like anyone, complexly layered.

---

[142] Hafsa Qureshi, "Too Queer to Be Muslim, Too Muslim to Be Queer," News.Trust.org, February 25, 2019.

These biases aren't just held by those outside of the Muslim community and the LGBTQ+ community. Qureshi herself has to continuously work to overcome them.

"Queer brown people didn't exist. If they did, the earth must have swallowed them whole as soon as they came out because I had never met any."[143] Hafsa couldn't figure out how to make herself fit into the two molds she saw before her, that of the devoted Muslim and the proud bisexual.

In her blog, Hafsa recounts relying on stereotypes and seeking out signs that someone else in her vicinity might also be LGBTQ+, or at least questioning their sexual identity. "There was that guy in school who seemed queer, or that one girl who *seemed* to stare when other girls changed in physical education. Maybe they were straight, maybe they weren't. But on paper, there could be no anomalies."[144]

Hafsa loved learning about Islam, praying, and wearing the hijab. Realizing she was attracted to women as well as men made her question if she may be forced to give up an essential part of who she was—her faith.[145]

So, she fought the cultural expectation. She did her own research and found the stories of strong, effective women in Islamic history. She found women who were the heads of armies, those who were strategic in business and making positive change in their communities. She realized the

---

143 Qureshi, 2019.
144 Qureshi, 2019.
145 Hafsa Qureshi, "Too Queer to Be Muslim, Too Muslim to Be Queer," News.Trust.org, February 25, 2019.

status-quo expectation of her gender performance and its implied straightness was not necessarily based in religion but a tool of control by wider society.[146]

Hafsa's Twitter presence has sent me down fantastic Google-holes about Khawla bint Al Azwar, disability advocacy as an LGBTQ+ person, and modern-day experiences of Ramadan.[147] Her voice is stern, knowledgeable, and educational in a matter-of-fact way that asserts her own space. It's content worth following for updated ally-ship and LGBTQ+ education.

Hafsa has written about the irritation that comes from people constantly commending her for being "different," for being "brave" and "breaking stereotypes." LGBTQ+ and non-LGBTQ+ people have turned her queerness into something political. Her bisexuality was used to separate her from her Muslim roots, not to celebrate the diversity that can be born within them.[148]

She is, of course, not alone in this scramble to figure out where and if her identities can align. In other parts of this book, the strength and pride born from community comes up over and over again. This connection to community is not exclusive to the queer community for LGBTQ+ people. Many of us also want to maintain the love and celebration we feel from the communities we were part of even before coming out as LGBTQ+. The cultural myths that faiths such as Islam and Christianity are unable to support

---

146 Qureshi, 2019
147 "Feminist Muslim Warrior Series: Khawla Bint Al Azwar, The Muslim Mulan." The Odyssey Online, October 17, 2019.
148 Qureshi, 2019.

LGBTQ+ people are honestly terrifying for people raised in these religious traditions. Like with the efforts of Qureshi, there are organizations designed to help LGBTQ+ people connect with others in the same faith and locate welcoming religious communities.

The Trevor Project has a guide called "Coming Out as You"[149] to help with these considerations. There is no rush to come out and no one should make LGBTQ+ people feel they need to be out to any individuals or groups of people. It's just like any other identifier and similar to faith in that the level of visibility is flexible.

The Institute for Welcoming Resources[150] is the most comprehensive and up-to-date website devoted to providing religious and faith-based resources for the LGBTQ+ community. (It visually reads as Christian, in my opinion, but contains resources for a variety of faiths.)

Something I brought up earlier in this book is worth pointing out again, here. Stay safe. Make room. As LGBTQ+ people are considering whether or not to come out, the most crucial element is both mental and physical safety and comfort with being out. The big traditional religions do not, as most people practice them, encourage violence. This does not prevent rogue people within them from speaking with cruelty or, more commonly, using "saving" language as a way to make LGBTQ+ people feel as though their chosen religious

---

149 Fishberger, Jeffrey, Phoenix Schneider, and Henry Ng. "Coming Out as You." The Trevor Project, January 2017.
150 Bischoff, Meredith. "The Institute for Welcoming Resources." Accessed March 2020.

community will be unable to accept them until they perform as if they are straight and cisgender.

There are benefits and risks to coming out, and each individual has to study their environment to weigh the pros and cons, which can be exhausting. Letting the people in their religious groups know about this aspect of their identity is important because then they know they are loved, gender and sexuality included. This helps LGBTQ+ people feel less alone. But sometimes there are challenges to which both queer people and their allies need to pay attention.

In her blog, Hafsa quotes black lesbian activist Audre Lorde, asserting that

> "Survival is not an academic skill. It is learning how to stand alone, unpopular and sometimes reviled, and how to make common cause with those others identified as outside the structures in order to define and seek a world in which we can all flourish."[151]
>
> AUDRE LORDE

---

[151] Hafsa Qureshi, "Too Queer to Be Muslim, Too Muslim to Be Queer," News.Trust.org, February 25, 2019.

Hafsa Qureshi deals with what many other LGBTQ+ youth and adults have to manage. Various faiths and congregations have different views on the LGBTQ+ community. What she discovered is hard to grasp if someone has been taught differently their entire life, but she found that there is nothing wrong with being queer. She realized its normalcy and its natural presence within society, including Muslim society.[152] In fact, it is completely normal and natural. Many LGBTQ+ people are religious and continue to attend religious services, and the people who are out in these communities, even with the risks, make it increasingly possible for more people to find faiths that welcome their whole selves.

---

152 Qureshi, 2019.

FANFIC AS DISCOVERY

—

When Xany was twelve, she discovered fan fiction. "I was on the computer in the living room that my parents also shared, so it was like a lot of trying to be sneaky about what I was reading."

Xany's parents gave her more time on the computer than the other kids because, well, she was *reading*. In fan fiction, the foundations of the characters and story are already laid out.

This means that, while authors can change anything they don't view as useful from the original story, they are able to focus their writing on steamy plots and intrigue. Her favorite fan fiction stories to read were based on the Harry Potter books, and the magic of the originals seemed even more colorful and brighter in the remixed tales centered on the minor characters. She started with lots of fantastical short fiction, less than ten thousand words of non-canonical stories, works set between opposing characters Hermione and Draco, but soon also discovered smut fiction (more sexually explicit fan fiction), and drifted into reading queer-centered works around age thirteen.

Xany isn't alone. There are millions of stories on Fanfiction.net alone. Millions.

A handful of other young women at my Catholic girls' school and I frequently shared and discussed slash (man with man) fan fiction, often with smutty storylines. This fan fiction was a huge part of my own LGBTQ+ explorations and general sex education. It's not uncommon to come across slash fiction. I'd go so far as to say there is probably at least one short fiction work out there involving two canonically straight characters in a queer relationship for every dramatic show on television. I imagine this as similar to the television tropes where young boys discover and trade pornographic magazines. We experienced our sexual curiosities through inconsequential, fictional tales written by fans of the shows, books, and musical groups that we loved.

This queer slash fiction (femslash for women-with-women stories) can be traced back to fan magazines published in

1960s that went into saucy detail about the non-canonical romance between Star Trek's Captain Kirk and Spock.[153]

The broad and seemingly inescapable phenomenon of slash fiction may be confusing to those outside of the fandom, particularly because its authors and readers are usually made up of a lot of straight girls who enjoy reading about two guys together. Imagine the group of guys cheering over women making out at a college party. Fan fiction is a quieter version of the same kind of hyper-sexualization and objectification, but it can be educational and, luckily, it is usually based around fictional characters.

I recall reading Harry Potter and Draco Malfoy fan fiction. While it's definitely true that I was objectifying the characters, they opened my eyes to stories about LGBTQ+ discovery, coming out, consent, and valid non-hetero relationships. One story I read when I was thirteen years old specifically walked through a vignette of Draco realizing he hated Harry so much because he was actually *infatuated* with him. He proceeded to avoid Harry at all costs until the two ultimately ended up having sex on some magical moving stairs during a particularly supervisor-less detention period. I laugh thinking about this now, but I'm grateful that my early experiences reading about sex were nonviolent and cushioned by fiction. This kind of porn helped me to avoid developing unrealistic expectations around sex, save the ability to flick lights off with a wand.

---

153 Jenkins, Henry. "'Welcome to Bisexuality, Captain Kirk': Slash and the Fan-Writing Community." In Textual Poachers: Television Fans and Participatory Culture, 237–74. Routledge, 2013.

It's odd to think of me and my white-socked, makeup-free teenage friends discussing our favorite chapters from an elaborate fan fiction now. I understand that part of my life in a new light. For them, reading these stories was about something hot and new to their young brains. This was true for me, sure, but it was also about finding representation. Xany and I, before we ever knew each other, shared this experience of learning about sex and intimacy through the imagination of fellow book and movie franchise fans. I'm sure if it had not been written smut, I'd have consumed other sorts of pornography at that age anyway. Most people do discover sexually explicit content by the time they are eleven years old.[154] I don't know if I would have been able to come to any positive revelations about queer relationship forming and love, outside of the act of sex itself, because I did not have these examples taught in school. We weren't celebrating Ellen's wedding in my household. The books I was reading usually included teen girls crushing on apathetic boys. When I was finding these imagined tales born from straight narratives, I didn't even have side characters to look to who were openly LGBTQ+, especially not in media geared toward young people.

Don't misunderstand this story as a suggestion that this fan fiction—written by (mostly) straight, cisgender women—was an adequate introduction into queer love. Even non-pornographic stories and sources would fall a bit short if they weren't written by a member of the LGBTQ+ community. Claire Rudy Foster, a queer nonbinary trans writer, expertly

---

154 Jane Randel and Amy Sánchez. "Parenting in the Digital Age of Pornography," *HuffPost*, February 26, 2017.

points out that the fan fiction I grew up with represents not queer people but the imagined lives of queer people.[155] Particularly the Draco and Harry stories I mentioned fetishized these characters as objects of curiosity imbued with the gay-best-friend dynamic. Gay men weren't the intended audience of these stories. I was. Well, straight women were.[156] Had they tumbled into the femslash fiction universe I later gravitated toward, I wonder if they'd be as interested in "queer representation." It's one thing to enjoy kinks and another to claim any sort of representation. I'm not hating on the fantasies, just hoping to point out that this early material I still view as somewhat educational is far from flawless.

When I was thirteen years old, I needed to see an episode of *Lizzie McGuire* or *Ned's Declassified School Survival Guide* where a kid my age was navigating a queer crush or who had gay parents. This wasn't available, so I fell into the hypersexual stuff. There were subtler stories, of course, but these were in the minority. Luckily, a total 10.2 percent of regular characters in the 2019-2020 broadcast television season are reported to be LGBTQ+, according to GLAAD's "Where We Are on TV" report (though asexuality got left out of this season of television).[157] This is up from 8.8 percent the prior season, so I hope that this positive influx will further impact kids' television.

---

155 Alanna Okun, "Why Are So Many Gay Romance Novels Written by Straight Women?" Electric Literature, March 21, 2019.
156 Okun, 2019.
157 Megan Townsend, "GLAAD's 'Where We Are on TV' Report Shows TV Is Telling More LGBTQ Stories than Ever." GLAAD, November 7, 2019.

Thinking back on it now, I am grateful I had friends who made me feel safe enough to swap fan fiction stories. That little community allowed me to see non-heteronormative relationships as something positive. Xany and my interest in these stories wasn't some gross plague of curiosity we needed to deny ourselves but little opportunities to think outside our usual, heteronormative lens.

CASSANDRA: FINDING COMMUNITY IN SUBTLETY

Growing up in the South, in many ways, isn't hugely different from growing up in other parts of the United States, particularly now. Bias lives everywhere, just as people do, and while the hope is that someday everyone can feel safe being out in any context, finding a community can be a struggle based on geography.

For Cassandra (she/her), part of living and working in the South means seeking community even when it isn't obvious—piecing things together from clues and signaling to folks that she is queer without outright saying it.

This book asserts a couple of things over and over again:

1. Safety is the priority.
2. And make room.

In some spaces you feel comfortable being out and others you need to create your own space. These two ideas will flow together for some people more easily than others, depending on a number of contexts and life factors.

The LGBTQ+ community is as diverse as wider humanity with a range of experiences and views that don't all align simply because of existing under the queer umbrella. This makes the community exciting and capable of growth, but it can also be confusing for young LGBTQ+ people trying to build their space with vocabulary that is new or unfamiliar to some.

Our friend Cassandra from the introduction of this book feels particularly accepted by people in their twenties, her own age group. She has dealt with biphobia and panphobia—older generations of lesbian and gay individuals who just wanted her to choose a side and straight people who would wrongly use her experience as evidence that queerness is a choice. Even current movements, like the LGBTQ+ movement, are anchored in some old, traditional ideas, and these views are not just held by older members within the community but also some of the younger members they can influence.

"For example, my boss is progressive. My work has an explicit policy that you can't be fired for your sexual orientation. That's considered progressive. Anyway, he's older, and he's been in the art world for a long time. So, he's had to deal and become comfortable with the LGBTQ+ community, but when he was reviewing a resume from someone who he knew from a previous year, he was like, 'Oh, right. This is the person with pronouns.' And someone else said, 'Yeah, they use they and them pronouns.' And he scoffed, 'Ah, yeah. That's a hassle. And that's grammatically incorrect.'" He has since gotten better about this, apologizing for misgendering his staff, which gives Cassandra hope for his case, though she wished people would be more quickly accepting.

At the time of his biased remarks, all Cassandra could think about was how she'd been so sure this man was a safe person to interact with, how he would be affirming of her identity. "How can you be so cool with gay people, but using a different pronoun is somehow something you aren't down with?" In Cassandra's mind, celebrating the LGBTQ+ community shouldn't have to be something that comes in steps.

"It's not like, 'Okay, I've accepted gay people. Now, I can move on to bi people, and then I can move on to trans people.' We should accept everyone all at once." That's what inclusion means, right? There should be no weird, tiered acceptance system.

I could sense Cassandra shaking her head over the phone while she told me,

"I feel like a lot of people are super proud of being L's (lesbian) or G's (gay), but then they don't actually also want to be an ally to the rest of the LGBTQ+ alphabet. Everyone should be an ally to each other."

Cassandra did eventually find peers who were truly both LGBTQ+ and allies to the community at work. Prior to her current job, she found a small group of people at her office who weren't out as queer in general because of the culture of the office but were out with each other.

"We really got to know each other while we were there. And part of it was that the office was just such a terrible environment that we all kind of clung to each other, just out of desperation." This wasn't the best circumstances under which to forge community, but many people benefit from being able to find solace in one another when facing stress. Cassandra was able to out herself subtly, "I think one of my coworkers knew the other was bisexual, and as I became closer friends with them it just sort of came up. It wasn't a big conversation. We were talking about undergrad or something because I was pretty out when I was in college, which was nice."

This story holds examples of many ways in which queer people are made to feel as if they need to self-censor or remove particular aspects of their identity from conversations. Cassandra was able to be out at work, but only to particular individuals. Even in her other post, where her boss was an ally, she felt he would judge any queer person who didn't suit his views on what the LGBTQ+ community should be.

According to reports collected by Catalyst.org:

- 22 percent of LGBTQ+ Americans have not been paid equally or promoted at the same rate as their peers.
- 53 percent of LGBTQ+ employees heard lesbian and gay jokes at work, while 37 percent heard bisexual jokes and 41 percent heard transgender jokes in 2018.
- 46 percent of LGBTQ+ workers in the United States are closeted in the workplace.
- 59 percent of non-LGBTQ+ employees believe it is "unprofessional" to discuss sexual orientation or gender identity in the workplace.
- 10 percent of LGBTQ+ employees have left a job because the work environment did not accept LGBTQ+ people.[158]

Stories like Cassandra's are common. Even those who are part of the LGBTQ+ community often make it difficult for their peers to feel comfortable bringing their whole selves into the workplace. No one is arguing that detailed information about coworkers' sex lives need to be shared. What matters is that the office Christmas party isn't made tense if someone brings a same-gender partner. Pronouns shouldn't be an inconvenience. If my friend's six-year-old can remember to use they and them without scoffing, a grown man should be able to do the same. These learned ideas are actively preventing queer people from accessing higher positions, forming baseline friendships at work, and even staying in their jobs.

---

[158] "Lesbian, Gay, Bisexual, and Transgender Workplace Issues: Quick Take," Catalyst.org, June 17, 2019.

Stigma and methodological barriers have made researching the community difficult. Accurate counts of the lesbian, gay, bisexual, and transgender populations (it is worth noting that other people under the queer umbrella are often left uncounted) are skewed because some surveys only measure the number of people in same-gender couples.[159] This removes single LGBTQ+ people and bi, pan, and queer people in straight-presenting or fluid relationships from the studies.

LGBTQ+ people have been finding community in subtlety for a long time. Cassandra was lucky enough to have people in her office who were out at work and were open enough to risk discussing workplace issues amongst themselves. But what about outside of work?

"I sometimes present a little differently, maybe 'more gay,' in certain spaces. I have a friend who told me that their roller-derby team had queer folks in it. With those roller derby people, for example, I wanted to be able to signal that I was also queer. When we are out, the people around can pick up on clues. So I'll start the evening thinking, 'Okay, well, let me put on a flannel, and let me roll up my jeans a little bit.' And, 'God, I hope my hair is not too "normy," and my nails aren't too long.'"

There's a list of disadvantages and privileges that comes both with being perceivably a member of a community, and less perceivably so. Stereotyping is dangerous in some circumstances, but for people like Cassandra, attempting to look the

---

159 Hansi Wang, "2020 Census Will Ask about Same-Sex Relationships," *NPR*, March 30, 2018.

part can be exhausting. "I'm just going to have to tell people I'm bi because they're not going to pick up on it enough because I don't seem queer enough." We talked about how this may be more difficult for women because a man who is remotely effeminate is often marked as queer while a woman could present any stereotypical gender presentation under the sun and still be understood as straight. Basically, society seems to think everyone must want to sleep with men. "I feel like most people have an image of a stereotypical, gay male, and to a certain extent, lesbians as well. Which is debatably not useful, but it is true. For folks who don't present as these stereotypes, the cues are small. If you're in the community, you know what these things are. But if you're not, you don't." It's just hard meeting new people, even to have a romantic relationship with, because cultural signals can be so unreliable and messy. Cassandra's current girlfriend resorted to asking her if she was going to Pride to try to figure out if she was LGBTQ+ because she couldn't tell. We take so much from visual cues that it can be hard to balance when to lean in to stereotypes in order to find community.

"On TikTok, I've seen people will have two fingernails on their hands filed down (for sex involving hands and vulvas). And that's a pretty obvious sign, but if I'm not currently with a woman, I don't want my nails to look stupid. And then what do I do?"

The same tactics that help queer people find other queer people don't necessarily work for everyone. Part of the brilliance of this community is its diversity, but that also makes heteronormativity a more difficult monster to deal with because there is not a one-size-fits-all game plan for presenting one's place in the LGBTQ+ community. There is no real rainbow mating call. As difficult as it can be to find ways to weave in queerness at work without being deemed "unprofessional," it can be just as hard to find friends and potential partners in spaces that aren't specifically deemed as queer. Despite these obstacles, once one is able to build even a small community, they flourish.

"Getting a sense of community is a really important thing. That has meant so much to me. I went too long not understanding who I was because I didn't have any LGBTQ+ people in my life. There were no out people in the media and there was no one to talk to about it because I wasn't gay. I wasn't straight. In my head, all the time, I said, 'So what do I do with this?' So, getting a sense of community and that feeling of, 'It's okay, you're figuring it out, and that's okay. We're here for you,' was so important."

Bisexuals exist. We aren't unicorns. And discovering other people and having community, whether that's online or over a book or in human form, even only subtly, makes a huge of difference.

KASH: COMING OUT TWICE

—

"I realized I was queer, or into girls, during my freshman year of college. I had subconsciously known before that, but I went to a private high school where being into women would not have been acceptable, so I just shoved that feeling down." While Kash (they/them) thought they were a boy in third and fourth grade, they repressed that feeling until senior year of college. There, they identified as a lesbian because that was the available language for them. While they were able to avoid managing these realizations in high school, these perceptions became more difficult to ignore once Kash went to college.

Kash is a trans nonbinary Lebanese-American designer and a sneaker-head based in Washington, DC. I met Kash and their partner, Kim, in my graduate school program and was quickly drawn to their humor and general creative energy. After briefing these two friends on the premise for this book and devouring delicious arepas together, I asked Kash how they started to figure out that the gender binary that is still so ingrained into American society today didn't suit them.

"My roommate was a lesbian. And my reaction was, 'Oh, that's cool. Interesting.' And then we ended up dating for two and a half years." Kash and Kim both laughed at the matter-of-fact tone in Kash's voice.

When I pushed for a little more information on how that relationship was able to form so quickly, Kash said, "I had a crush on my Spanish teacher, who was a woman, and I think meeting my roommate, finally knowing someone my age who was also interested in women, was helpful in my acknowledgment of this big thing I had known for a while."

Kash hadn't felt a crush like this before, so they ventured to Google, as many young people do when trying to figure out their sexual identity, and found lesbian porn. "I went in just thinking, 'Let's see if I'm disgusted by this,' and then immediately, 'I am NOT, in fact, disgusted by this.' So, I guess that crush warmed me up to the idea of dating women."

When Kash started dating their roommate, Olivia, the couple became the "lesbians on the floor," attention that Kash wasn't excited about. But Kash did not have a panicked moment around being queer, just a concern that their relationship would be discussed without their knowledge. "It was just kind of awkward. If we hadn't been living together it wouldn't have been as weird, but it just kind of happened."

After they started dating Olivia, Kash began dressing more feminine. "For some reason, I didn't want to be this lesbian stereotype, even though I don't even know if I thought of myself as a lesbian." Kash made sure to have long hair and wear makeup and they "just did the literal most because I didn't want to be butch." (Butch is a term often used by people both within and outside of the LGBTQ+ community to mean someone with a very masculine appearance. I love a video by the publisher *them.* on this topic called "Butch Women Talk About What It Means to Be Butch.")[160]

But by Kash's senior year of college, they started getting uncomfortable with this form of gendered presentation. "I didn't like wearing the clothes I had been wearing. If I had to wear a dress for a presentation, I'd have an absolute breakdown and just think over and over, 'I hate this.'"

Soon, Kash began to dress "sportier," particularly in casual settings. As we chat, I notice Kash's upcycled sweatpants with a very cool ridged pattern they added themself to the black pants. For as long as I had known Kash, they have dressed in street-style fashions with a confidence that lent itself to their nonbinary expression. It can be difficult to describe clothes outside of "masculine" and "feminine," though clothes themselves do not require gender.

---

160 "Butch Women Talk about What It Means to Be Butch." *Them.* YouTube, 2017.

After enduring a different, difficult relationship and moving to DC to begin grad school, Kash became so uncomfortable with their remaining feminine items of clothing and presentation that it began to affect their mentality around health and school. "I was just so uncomfortable all the time, and I was talking to my ex on the phone because I wasn't sleeping. It was just terrible. I had gained a ton of weight and I did not understand what was wrong with me. I was in the middle of saying, 'I just feel so uncomfortable all the time,' and she just said, 'You're trans.'" Kash nods and laughs at the absurdity of how straightforward the statement was, "and I was like, 'Yep. I am.'"

Often friends can be rightfully nervous about asking sexuality or gender, and to a large extent, being cautious about not outing someone or even making assumptions about them in the first place is a good practice to have. In Kash's case, however, someone else needed to say it for them. Kash's ex, by stating what she believed was the cause of Kash's discomfort, was able to give permission for Kash to *really* start researching what their unease meant.

"I watched a ton of YouTube videos to try to figure out exactly how I felt and if other people were feeling that way." Kash's ex walked them through their definition of trans, asking questions like, "Do you feel uncomfortable when people call you she?" And after these conversations and a month-long YouTube rabbit hole, Kash landed on using "they" and "them." They also got really into fashion and design, tailoring their own pieces to suit their body the way they wanted since most men's clothing off the rack was too large or shaped too broadly.

"It feels better. And it's not a good feeling. Being nonbinary is not a good feeling because nothing ever feels *quite* right, but I do feel a lot better when people address me as 'they' because then I don't have to pretend I'm a woman. I'm not a good actor."

Though being trans nonbinary carries some frustrations, its acknowledgment also comes with some transgender liberation moments, like choosing a new name. Kash crowdsourced name ideas from their group of friends, asking if certain names fit them and focusing on finding a Middle-Eastern name with which they would vibe well.

"I went through a lot of baby name books online." Kash smiles and picks at the pills on their *Supreme* sweatshirt. "I found Kashir and that was pretty unanimously liked. A couple of people thought Kash sounded like a stage name, but I'm not trying to work for the government, so whatever."

Kashir is a man's name, but most Americans don't understand its origins. Kash was particularly attracted to its meaning—humorous man. "I feel like I'm kind of a goof, so it fit."

As we moved from arepas to Kim's fantastic banana bread, I asked Kash about the relationship between their gender identity and their sexuality. A, another gender nonbinary friend I interviewed for this book, introduced me to the fact that people have a hard time calling themselves "gay" or "lesbian" if they, themselves, don't identify as a man or a woman. Kash confirmed this experience, using queer as their language, though they are only sexually attracted to women.

"I was so established in my sexuality at that point because it had been maybe four or five years since I initially came out as queer. Some people realize they're trans and register their sexuality simultaneously, but who I'm attracted to didn't change when I realized I was trans." I asked Kash if they wish there was a word that better encompassed their identity. "No, I don't think I care that much. I think labels are helpful when you're first coming out and so other people can understand you. But, who I'm attracted to depends on so many things, so I don't feel like there needs to be more specific words than queer."

Kash's story is important for many reasons, but the fact they came out to their parents twice for two conversations—about their preference for women and then about their gender—and the methods they used to do it are crucial to the current LGBTQ+ conversation. First, during undergrad, Kash had to announce their relationship with Olivia.

"It was Thanksgiving break and my parents and I had this leftover turkey we were putting into Tupperware. And I started the conversation by saying, 'You know how you both said you'd love me no matter what?'" Kash's parents had known Olivia, but really just as Kash's roommate—at least that's what Kash thought. Then Kash said, "Olivia and I are together." And everything got quiet. Kash's dad, on the brink of tears said, "We know." They were both perceptive people. Kash told me they had likely hoped they were wrong. Kash had been acting weird and had been texting and FaceTiming with Olivia more than most people would with their roommate on their first Thanksgiving break. When I asked how Kash got hyped up to even have that conversation, they said. "I was, well, I mean… I was scared shitless both times."

When Kash decided to come out to their parents as transgender nonbinary a couple of years later, the choice came after a scare where their parents showed up to their apartment early before Kash could hide the boxers and masculine clothes lingering around the room. Kash, at this point in graduate school, had gotten into the habit of removing items like this before their parents would show up. After this small panic, Kash went to their therapist and insisted that they needed their parents to know about their gender-identity. Kash wrote a letter that said all they wanted to say, read it to their therapist, and then called their parents and asked them not to speak until the letter was fully read aloud.

"I guess they may just know me better than I always think they know me, so they can tell when something's up." Kash explained that while their parents weren't happy about their nonbinary gender, they also weren't wholly surprised. They also haven't quite adopted using Kash's pronouns yet. "I guess when you have a kid, you picture their life a certain way, so when the kid is like, 'Nope!' it's an adjustment." Kash felt like they had been hiding so much. They had it in their head that they'd already "disappointed" their parents by telling them they were queer, and they didn't want to make the situation worse. "It's one thing to be, you know, attracted to women, but another to be like 'I'm not a woman.'"

Kash made sure to practice reading the letter to their best friend, Kerin, and to their therapist before reading it to their parents over the phone. "Kerin was like, 'Oh, I love it!' Shout

out to Kerin. And so, I went back to therapy the next week and read it and she was like…" Kash scrunched up their face dramatically reenacting the emotion in the therapist's face and cries of pride.

"I usually call them every night or every other night, so I called them right after therapy and read the letter. I still have it." Kash took immediate control of the conversation, asking their parents to listen carefully without responding until the letter was completely read all the way through. According to Kash, their mom's response after a few moments of silence was, "I don't know what the hell the big deal is!" and when Kash asked, "What?" she said, "Well, I mean, if you want to wear men's clothes and stuff that's okay, whatever." So maybe not totally getting it, but the conversation definitely could have gone worse. Kash has been showing documentaries and YouTube videos during their visits, "just to explain shit. There's science behind this. I didn't just decide to do this, to be this way."

Kash is a self-proclaimed person-who-gives-good-advice-but-doesn't-take-it and wishes they were better about correcting people when the wrong pronouns are used to refer to them. "I just get super nervous, but when I first came out, I was much better about it for some reason." Kash was great about letting their professors know to use they and them pronouns early on, but they got nervous when some professors would seem confused. At one point, a professor asked Kash individually to explain what they meant by their pronouns and the conversation, which seemed scary on the surface, but turned out to be a really pleasant and important.

> "He basically asked, 'How can I make the class more inclusive for people?' and I told him to ask for people's pronouns for the first class. I explicitly said, 'Don't say preferred pronouns—just say pronouns because they're not preferred.' And he was really receptive."

In addition to the right pronouns, Kash let their professors know that their voice, the pitch of it, upsets them "because I feel like it's very high, so sometimes participating is hard for me because I don't want to talk in front of other people." Kash assured their professors that they would come to class well prepared, but that they spent more time thinking about what they'd say because of the added presentation aspect of needing to speak aloud. Each professor Kash has had this conversation with has been accepting because, really, what could they say to the contrary? Professors are there to support student learning, and Kash's experience serves as a great example of how to take a little time to make sure professors are getting things right. "I think some people just need a little explaining. If you normalize it and are persistent, it'll be okay."

For a "discomfort" project in grad school, Kash and their peers were tasked with doing something they'd been putting off for a long time or something that generally just made them uncomfortable—ideally, something productive they would feel happy about once it had been done. So, Kash decided to search for a suit. "At this point, for formal stuff, I only have dresses, and I don't want to fucking wear a dress. I couldn't actually find a suit that fit me that wasn't $1,000 to customize. I did find dress pants that looked great, so that was fine."

When the time came to present about the discomforts in class, Kash found themselves standing up and, instead of talking about the suit, came out to their sixty-plus-person graduate seminar. "I was like, 'Am I going to do this? I guess I'm doing this.'" Kash stated matter-of-factly that they were trans nonbinary and that their pronouns were they and them. Everyone clapped and the professor of the course even said something along the lines of, "Damn, I guess this assignment really works." With a frustrated but humorous smile, Kash told me people basically ignored their pronouns after this big event, but the experience felt really good nonetheless.

"I feel like the people who care will make the effort, not that it is really any effort. In that moment I was like, 'Wow, *I* really did that.' I don't like that kind of attention. It makes me super nervous, but I couldn't expect people to gender me correctly if I didn't *tell* them what to use."

And these conversations don't necessarily have to be a "big deal." Subtle corrections can be just as useful. When Kash was recently at a Halloween party, they met a new friend who kept referring to them with she and her pronouns. Kim, Kash's partner, continued the conversation with ease but made sure to firmly refer to Kash with the correct they and them pronouns. The new friend caught on pretty quickly and adjusted accordingly. No pain, no strain, honestly no effort really at all. This shift allowed Kim to correct this person without anyone becoming embarrassed or confused. Because really, it isn't that hard to hear what people say and think to use their pronouns. It's just like using their names.

This coming into self has allowed Kash to realize their goals and ambitions. Kash had gone down a pretty specific path to become a diplomatic translator and loved languages but realized they did not want to work in a serious environment. Coming into their full self allowed them to acknowledge this, and they started Customs by Kash, an UpCycling and Design company. "Now that I'm being honest with myself about who I am, let me be honest with myself about what I want to do." Because each step of discovering your true self helps guide you to discovering the whole.

ALAYNA: WHY STIR THE POT?

Alayna Joy (she/her) built a career and a massive online following out of fun, educational YouTube content. She, like Kash, has had the experience of coming out multiple times, though these announcements were considerably more public. She announced she was bisexual on her channel back in 2015, with a very fun Draw-My-Life style video.[161]

---

161 "Draw My Life (Coming Out)," Alayna Joy, YouTube, 2015.

In May of 2020, she re-came out, updating her audience to the fact that she is actually gay (used as an umbrella term by some non-straight folks and people who are attracted to their same and similar genders).[162] Much of her queer journey was similar to mine, and finding her content when I was in high school helped me to feel considerably less alone. In follow-up social media posts after her "Coming Out Again" video, Alayna seemed surprised at how her audience quickly accepted her gay identity after so much of her content was centered around bisexuality, but I think this embracing of updates and discovery makes this new generation of LGBTQ+ people so incredible.[163] Alayna's gayness doesn't change her place as an important, accessible queer person in my life, and this likely applies to the rest of her audience as well.

I chatted on the phone with Alayna back in November of 2019, and thankfully I hadn't mixed up her Canadian time zone with mine in DC. We laughed and agreed about many similar experiences as women who are attracted to women. She told me, "I assumed all women felt the same way I did and we just didn't talk about it." Yep. I remember the first time a girl in high school mentioned how weird she thought lesbians were and I could not comprehend how anyone could not find women *so attractive*.

Alayna grew up in a small, conservative town. "I had always been taught that gay is bad and you're going to hell. Straight is what's good. So, I assumed my feelings toward women

---

162 Ashley Mardell, *The ABC's of LGBT+*. (Mango Media Inc, 2016.), 9.
163 "The wedding is off. | Coming Out Again," Alayna Joy, YouTube, 2020.

were how we all just experience friendship. This is how women connect. This is how we feel about each other." It wasn't until Alayna was nineteen, when she first heard the word bisexual on YouTube, that she realized this element of her identity was not universal. "I remember it shaking my entire world. I had to go back through my whole history, back to junior high school—all of my experiences, and all of my relationships—to rewrite my own understanding of my history."

Going by the username Alayna Joy on YouTube, Alayna makes videos covering topics like mental health, sexuality, and veganism. I came across her posts before she was out, and I was thrilled when she actually made her initial coming out video. She served as one of my main representatives on the platform of what it can look like to be proud to be queer and also in a "straight-presenting" relationship.

In the description box of her "Coming Out Again" video, Alayna states, "This is a hard video for me to make, but I need you to know the truth. I'm gay. I don't know what this means for my future, but I hope you'll stick with me as I figure it out." A huge element of what made this so difficult was because the realization that she was gay meant she and her male partner separated. Going through any breakup is hard, but Alayna realized it is possible to truly love someone's presence and companionship and confuse that genuine love for romantic and sexual love. Added external pressures of heteronormativity and fears about being a "fake-bisexual-stereotype" (an inaccurate idea that bisexuality is just a stepping stone to being gay) made it even more difficult for Alayna to realize that she was gay.

In our conversation, Alayna told me that when she was young, she had labeled a close friendship, a best friendship with a woman, as just that—platonic. When she realized it had been so much more than that for both parties, she had to re-evaluate that whole relationship. "It was romantic. I had to look back at that friendship and go, 'Oh, this experience was a relationship.' And when it ended without clarity, I hadn't realized we had basically been together, so when I started dating someone else, that wasn't okay." You can hear Alayna go into this a bit more in her video, "Draw My Life (Coming Out) | MissFenderr."[164]

Before she made this video, she and her then-boyfriend, Sam*, had been on and off throughout school. "We were both figuring things out, but we'd been together for about two years. When I came out to him, he was wonderful and supportive. And I honestly thought I'd never have to talk about it again because this very important person in my life now knew and was accepting."

But after a couple more years went by, Alayna felt herself growing restless and not recognizing why. "I had just been trying to repress and basically shut that part of myself away, which didn't work. It came to a point where I was thinking about it all the time. So, I came out to him again." Her partner was originally worried that this conversation meant Alayna did not want to be with him anymore, but after her assurance that she did love him, she just also needed to be open and honest, he was increasingly supportive. In her most recent video, Alayna describes knowing that she did love Sam

---

[164] "Draw My Life (Coming Out)," Alayna Joy, YouTube, 2015.

and that the two, together, had decided back in 2015 that if she was really interested in women but did want to be with him, she must be bisexual. In actuality, however, she was gay but did not want to lose Sam from her life. That relationship was, and still is, real and important. Changing the nature of this relationship, now, is likely something that will take adjustment, communication, and time, but Alayna seems so relieved in her latest video—hurt by these experiences but relieved to have allowed herself to realize who she is and no longer have to hide. The two are figuring out how to build a beautiful friendship.

"He was the one who said to me, 'This is a part of your life. This is a part of who you are. You don't ever have to feel like you can't talk about this with me.'"

Ingrid Nilson, another YouTube content creator, had come out as gay on the platform not too long before Alayna's 2015 video and set an example for the ways online communities often embrace their favorite creators' sexual and gender identities.

"I saw her video and I basically had a breakdown. I kept thinking, 'I can't keep this quiet and I don't have to.'" At this point, Alayna wasn't ashamed of being queer but thought 'Why stir the pot? Why risk upsetting people when I'm already with the person who I know I want to be with for the rest of my life?' Alayna's answer, like mine, was that sexuality and romanticism can be an important element of identity. Had I seen people with this experience be vocal, either online or in person, I would not have felt shame for as long as I did. I would not have removed myself from the LGBTQ+ groups

I felt drawn to out of fear of being inauthentic or labeled as confused. I would have solidified more friendships and taken political actions without constantly questioning my rights to do so.

Alayna was afraid to head back home after posting her initial coming out as bisexual video. Her parents frequently had friends over, and Alayna wasn't sure how they would all respond to her online announcement in real life. "I remember walking in and everybody was outside, but one of my mom's friends was in the house. She walked straight up to me, she gave me a huge hug, and told me that she thought what I had just done was incredible." This explicit acceptance from someone outside of the family was powerful. This helped her to be less fearful and begin to *expect* positive reactions wherever she could.

> "I had this large desire for community, and this desire to just be myself, even if it meant nothing changed. It meant I wasn't hiding and I could speak about my experiences publicly without being afraid of who would find out."

I am so glad that now, months after our conversation, Alayna is continuing to be honest with her community, even when it is difficult.

She built most of this community online. "I knew a few queer people from my life back when I was in Winnipeg, right when I was coming out. But I didn't have a lot of access at all. Through YouTube, and through making friends online, I started to build that space." Since moving to Vancouver, Alayna has made a real point to try and find a queer community. She started this process online as well, reaching out to different people on Twitter, simply suggesting a meetup. "Slowly over the past few years, I've built and am still building this community."

Alayna's YouTube series, "I Don't Bi It," is a hilarious hit, pointing out the weird and ridiculous anti-LGBTQ+ arguments some people will make, all in a sarcastic tone. "The response was just overwhelmingly positive. And the people, the few people who didn't get it, did watch it, so they received all this informal information. Its design is a win-win." Even those who don't understand the joke are hearing answers to their own biases and questions. They're being educated either way.

Alayna has also been successful in more serious productions. She made a film for Buffer Festival, something far out of her comfort zone, and cites this project as one of the most rewarding she has ever made. "I got to build on many other stories that had been sent to me for this purpose, creating a story from many submitted narratives, which is something I want to continue doing on my YouTube channel and what I try to do with 'I Don't Bi It' as well." Alayna continues to use her platform to share other people's stories, making sure to invite as many voices onto her channel as she can and prioritizing open conversations over lectures.

"There are still many people within the LGBTQ+ community who still feel alone and you still don't have any sort of community. So, the only person they feel they have to talk to is somebody they've seen on the internet who they know won't judge them. It can be heavy to be that person, but it's an incredible position." Like LGBTQ+ representation in media, only having one source as a representative doesn't work. Platforms that allow search criteria based on multiple identifiers are particularly useful. I found Alayna when I was seeking bisexual content. Others may benefit from seeking LGBTQ+ and disabled voices, queer and Asian voices, and so on. There are thousands of possible combinations of identity, and Alayna found herself in a position where she could add her voice.

She still finds herself discovering small forms of self-acceptance that can be worked into an everyday ritual. "For me, clothing has been a big part of my identity journey. I can think of moments when I've looked in the mirror and see the way that I feel internally reflected in that mirror, through my clothing. And that's kind of playing with masculine and feminine. I like the way I feel more comfortable in a sports bra, something that kind of flattens my chest, just because I feel more comfortable with a more androgynous torso. I feel so much more like myself in a T-shirt, so getting rid of the push-up bras felt more like me. I've also always hated my hands, but now that I don't paint my nails and I keep them short, and I'm much more confident about them."

The balance and options and willingness to explore is really freeing for Alayna. She still loves to wear something lacy on occasion or look pretty for events, but letting go of the pressure to present herself fully done-up and wholly feminine all the time has helped her find internal validation—something I would argue is more important than that of others. "I also think getting older is helping. I'm becoming more comfortable with myself and having more moments of 'I am who I am, and nobody can take that away from me.'"

Toward the end of our conversation, I asked Alayna about a time when she felt truly validated in her queer identity. She shared a story about her first Pride after she had initially come out as bisexual.

Alayna went to Pride for the first time, after she'd come out initially, with her best friend. "We walked in the march together, side by side, and she held my hand. It seems like such a small thing, but for me, that really helped me to feel out and proud. I was surrounded by other people who were a part of the community." Alayna felt acceptance and love from her friend's hand, her willingness to be assumed as coupled with Alayna. "To also have that moment, to be able to express that part that side of myself, was something I'll never forget." I know she will continue to find this kind of validation, support, and love after coming out again.

Why stir the pot? Alayna's re-coming out was another huge "stirring the pot" moment, "and I think it's an important message to share that being who you are, being authentically you, is always worth the risk of stirring the hypothetical pot. (If you are safe to do so, of course.) It might be the most vulnerable and scary thing a person can do, but being your truest self is the most freeing thing a person can do. And in turn, you give others permission to do the same."

KIM: YOUR IDENTITY IS YOURS

Throughout high school, Kimberly Marcela Duron (she/her) was so focused on dance that she didn't date much, but she recalls being "very drawn" to a young woman in her classes who was an out and proud lesbian. "She [the lesbian] turned down another dancer in that program for a date because that dancer identified as bisexual. That rubbed me the wrong way." Kim internalized this bias, something that many young queer people do after witnessing anti-bi, pan, or queer behaviors from proud lesbian and gay individuals, as well as those outside of the LGBTQ+ community.

An Adam and Eve study found that 39 percent of men said they were open to dating a bisexual person, while 31 percent of women said they were; 15 percent of men versus 23 percent of women were unsure if they would date a bisexual person. The study did not ask for sexual orientation, but this depicts the subtlety of biphobia (and panphobia) where bisexual women are objectified, assumed to *really* be straight, and bisexual men are assumed to *really* be gay.[165] Negative assumptions around promiscuity and attention-seeking have hurt the queer community as a whole, diminishing internal collaboration and strength. Plenty of longitudinal studies have debunked these myths over and over again, but these stereotypes are hard to shake.[166]

Kimberly and I met our first year of grad school and connected over our passion for visual media storytelling. She identifies as queer, but this is a somewhat new development in her life, as her language around sexual identity did not form to this shape until she began dating Kash, the wonderful person who shared their experiences in this book in earlier pages. Kim made sure I was enjoying the mimosas and arepas she had prepared for brunch prior to our interview and, after we finished eating, she proudly affirmed that her identities included queer, Honduran (and more broadly Central American), and Cyber-Feminist (a genre of contemporary feminism in which thinkers, coders, and media artists use technology to hack the patriarchy).[167]

---

165 J.R. Thorpe, "Why Won't Some People Date Bisexuals?" Bustle.com, September 8, 2016.
166 Samantha Joel, "3 Myths About Bisexuality, Debunked by Science," *Psychology Today*, May 22, 2014.
167 Izabella Scott, "How the Cyberfeminists Worked to Liberate Women through the Internet," Artsy, October 13, 2016.

"I grew up as a dancer in the performing arts world. I was always in more creative spaces, even as a child, and for some reason, which I can't really pin down, in these spaces there tends to be a bit more self-expression." Kim moved to Los Angeles with her mom when she was in eighth grade and quickly joined the musical theater crowd, which allowed her to meet folks very forward with and open about their various sexualities. "By my senior year of high school, there were even more people I knew who were gender fluid."

Kim had her "sexual awakening" while she was in college, which happens for many people, and all of these sexual encounters were with cisgender men. While she was experiencing these relationships, she also found herself gravitating toward lesbian porn, initially thinking she liked this because it tends to be less aggressive and much more catered to satisfying the needs of the woman in the situation. Kim started to take note of a shift, more awareness of the women in films, and she worked to stifle the feelings. Why? Well, she has a gay uncle. And his experience in her family, while not horrible, wasn't appealing.

"It's not the 'norm' in my family. We are immigrants from Honduras, and this is a predominantly Catholic or Christian culture. Everyone knows my gay uncle is gay, but we don't *talk* about it."

When the family's romantic stories or gossip come up, the subject of her uncle's love life is avoided. His partners are not discussed. To Kim, growing up with this tension made it seem as if he wasn't a relevant member of the family. "It was not spoken about in the way that I wish it had been spoken about. I felt I had to be quiet on the topic."

Kim's mom, who was a psychology major in undergrad, had adopted a common school of thought that teaches that sexual trauma at a young age leads to sexual diversity in adulthood. In other words, she believes that LGBTQ+ people are LGBTQ+ because someone at some point hurt them.

"I can understand why people in previous generations, when it was even more stigmatized, would need a *reason*, but it's not helpful. So, unfortunately, I grew up with this mentality of my mom being very accepting and very loving and caring for the LGBTQ+ community, but for a sympathetic reason, not out of real approval."

Then, Kim went to graduate school and met Kash. The two were in a documentary film class together and were able to learn a lot about each other without hanging out, just the two of them, because each of their documentaries had their own personal identities as the center of their stories. "I was, again, very drawn to Kash and it brought up a lot of feelings about my past romantic relationships. Even when I had only engaged in sexual relationships with cis-het men (cisgender, heterosexual), they were all ridiculously different but creative. An artist, a designer, a musician, something like that. It had much more to do with who they were on the inside."

When Kim was grappling with her feelings toward Kash, she spoke to members of her "chosen family," a support system she found in friends in DC, about not having experience with folks who weren't men and her interest in Kash. Kevin, one of our peers in graduate school and a brilliant scholar and gay man from St. Louis, pointed out to Kim that "the person you're attracted to doesn't define your sexual identity." This statement removed some pressure from Kim, allowing her to be open to the idea of a relationship with Kash because it no longer meant she needed to radically transform the way she thought about her own sexual identity. What mattered would be her relationship.

"When Kash first asked me out, I actually said no because I knew it was going to have very big consequences, not in a negative way, but I knew it was going to take a lot of me, emotionally. And it was finals. The timing was pretty bad." Kim and Kash laughed together recalling this tale, and their care for one another is always so obvious when they are near one another. Despite Kim's original denial of a date, Kim and Kash texted every day that winter break, and the two found themselves working through family and friendship drama all while prioritizing and learning about one another. Kim almost missed out on this incredible relationship out of fear that she'd be stepping into a space she had no right to occupy, which just doesn't work for most queer individuals.

> "I had been very careful to consider what the line might be between someone wanting to experiment sexually versus really trying to get to know someone and being open to that identity shift."

Kim's knack for self-reflection was particularly important here. She was able to know the amount of work she'd need to do with herself to be the best partner for Kash and realize that her responsibility was in being open and loving, not in needing to fulfill some sort of gay standard.

Kash pulled up their text messages so they could recount how the relationship formed over the winter break. Watching the two blush together and laugh about how *millennial* the start of their connection had been—over text message—was adorable. And honestly, I think Kim serves as an awesome example of how to be queer and an ally all at once. She's constantly learning and checking in with both herself and with Kash to keep their communication strong.

"I was having conversations with Kevin that were just so eye opening. This idea that my sexual partner does not have to define my identity was such a foundational point. I was so nervous around labels and I really didn't need them. They're more for other people. I needed to prioritize *us*."

Kim is still working on boundaries with her family and has begun building a chosen family in addition to those she grew up with to be able to thrive in all of her known and undiscovered identities. "I had had the unfortunate experience with my mom outing me to other members of the family. But I was living with my uncle in Maryland, and he was so affirming." Though her uncle is from a different generation of the LGBTQ+ community, his perspective was not one of exclusion. One of Kim's aunts, Aunt Fanny, was also surprisingly supportive, simply saying, "I am so happy for you. I never want you to apologize or feel in any way like you're doing something wrong, because this is 100 percent normal." Even the tone she used with Kim was so reassuring, one of love and joy. Kim's happiness was her aunt's priority, and that is what real support looks like. She didn't love Kim *despite* her gender nonbinary partner but was thrilled her niece had found someone who loved and respected her in the way that she deserves.

So much of Kim's story asserts the ways good communication can be beneficial to any relationship. She worries sometimes that people will assume Kash converted her to the LGBTQ+ community, fulfilling the ever-present and hilarious idea of the "Gay Agenda," but she ultimately knows that, because of the love and support of her chosen family, she's queer and figuring it all out, and that is absolutely okay. More than okay. She continues diving into Latinx rights work, multimedia projects exploring how people of color are impacted by white ideals of beauty and does this with the support of someone who empowers and encourages her to continue to explore every element of herself. Kim mentioned quietly, smiling almost more to herself than to Kash or me, "I'm *so* happy."

BLAIR: EXPLORATION

"I remember one of the first video games where you got to have an option. There was a ninja game with a strong lady lead. I kept using her character, to the point where my friends basically said 'You can't use her anymore because you're too good.'"

Blair* (they/them) identifies as both nonbinary and queer. When I asked for their pronouns they, like how River discussed, said, "They and them is more accurate. Finding my identity was a bit twisty-turny." Blair started out believing they were a cisgender, bisexual man, but they never ruled out the possibility of adding, subtracting, or melding identities. "I have friends who can very confidently say, 'I'm straight,' but I can't do that." Blair, for as long as they can remember, has flirted with androgyny and felt more at home choosing more femme or androgynous characters.

When Blair was a young teenager, they did know about trans people but didn't learn about gender queer individuals until later. "I don't think being nonbinary was really in the lexicon yet. Since I didn't expressly feel trans, especially thinking about the process of transitioning physically, I did not feel that process was right for me. I don't feel like a woman."

Blair prefers to present as more androgynous, though sometimes this can be difficult. "I'll shave and then I have a five o'clock shadow the next day. I have hair from my head to my ankles." But instead of viewing the body hair and more traditionally "masculine" traits as a setback, Blair has just decided to broaden their conceptions of androgyny to include their own expressions and qualities.

"I had some dysphoria when I was eighteen about being so masculine looking. But eventually I just stopped shaving. I got more involved in a queer community that was accepting of different bodies." Blair has a close friend named Mimi, who uses she and her pronouns and also has a mustache.

> "I realized it's not so much about how you look. It's about how you present yourself. There are a whole lot of other ways to be androgynous."

Blair found much of their queer community by going to a singular party that opened doors for many more. One of their online friends invited them. Though this friend ended up not actually going, Blair made the point to go, and this opened their eyes to how easy making new friendships could be within the LGBTQ+ community. "I just continued going to these various queer parties and made friends, many to whom being nonbinary or trans was the norm."

Eventually, Blair was drawn to the kink community in New York. This opened up a whole new realm of questions, new types of (sex) parties, and helped Blair become a better communicator and reflective thinker. "In the kink community in New York, there are two spectrums. There's the very cis-spectrum, which can be a little… not explicitly unwelcoming, but honestly kind of creepy. And then there is the more queer side, which is hugely refreshing. Consent and safety and joy is prioritized there like no other community I've seen, though I've participated in both spectrums." While I have already mentioned in this book that queer communities are not inherently sexual, I do think the LGBTQ+ community has done a lot of work to stop shame around various kinks, which has benefitted loads of sexually active individuals, regardless of gender and sexual preference.

Blair has witnessed unsafe practices on the part of those getting into kink culture as a novelty outside of practiced communities. To help prevent injuries, Blair has acted as a sort of guard, a referee at sex parties, keeping everyone safe. Think hall pass badge, but much hotter. "Oh, it's very controlled. We try to keep people from combining it with alcohol and drinking. We turn people away when they're drunk or otherwise unable to consent."

Queer culture is not synonymous with kink culture and vice-versa, but presenting Blair's experiences is important to me because I think the hyper-sexualization of LGBTQ+ people comes from obsessions with binaries, bedrooms, and BDSM (bondage, discipline, sadism, and masochism—think *Fifty Shades* but way more consensual and fun). Straight, cisgender people partake in these events just as often as queer people, yet LGBTQ+ people are lumped together as if we all participate in every sort of sex act. I know some incredibly vanilla (a preference for conventional sex) queer people and some equally kinky straight couples, but often LGBTQ+ people are assumed to be the latter. Blair, unlike River, is into this. And that presents the intersectional, multi-layered element of the queer community. Sex, romance, gender—all of this looks different for everyone. Sex played an important role in Blair's attitude toward their own wants and desires. I think reflecting on this and exploring these ideas, especially outside of sex, can be useful for any adult figuring out how they want to live.

"I was able to stop looking at sex and intimacy in such a binary fashion, discovering a huge spectrum. And there isn't an assumption that I'd act with everybody in the same way. Just like everyone, we are attracted to some people and not to others, and that's completely fine. There are so many different enzyme and endocrine combinations that we just lump into broad categories of male and female." There are even a number of **intersex** (an umbrella term used to describe a wide range of natural bodily variations, some visible at birth, others at puberty) people who don't even know this about themselves because there may be no physical signs.[168]

In addition to scientific learning around sex, many people are still learning how to talk about gender. Rather than having everyone go in a circle announcing pronouns, Blair appreciates the thought but prefers a subtle approach that doesn't "other" the one or two trans, genderqueer, or nonbinary people in the room. "It would be great if we could just sign off as, instead of Mr. B or Miss W, we just use our initials or our names. In classes, I ask a person or two to use they for me and people usually slowly catch on."

The whole idea seems to stem from our collective desire to force people to categorize themselves. When I got married, I decided to keep my own name for many reasons. It's uncommon, it sounds nice, it suits me, and so on. It also bothers me that, culturally, the man is never asked to take his wife's name. Writing Mrs. Fredenburg, now, is irritating too. I'm not married to a person with the name Fredenburg. The "Mrs." is a totally unnecessary categorization that doesn't help me at all and further alienates people who don't identify with these titles. I do also, though, want to recognize that for some trans people, leaning into their true gender titles and pronouns can be freeing.

"Trans people are often forced to subvert the gender binary, but they can also find it comforting. Whereas genderqueer people are kind of just throwing it all to the wind. For us, it's

---

[168] Hida. "How Common Is Intersex? An Explanation of the Stats," Intersex Equality, April 1, 2015.

more of a rejection of the binary." The respect and eagerness to learn is something I see in Blair and hope to mirror in myself, especially as I continue to collect these stories. While some nonbinary people are asexual, some are polyamorous or into kinks or very subtle in the bedroom. But the ways we title ourselves (Mrs., Mr., kinky, vanilla, LGBTQ+, queer, etc.) are not the end-all-be-all of who we are. These labels are just a sign on the door to our experiences, and conversation is necessary for further understanding. That is surely more of an opportunity for continuous exploration.

ALEX:
WHAT WOULD YOUR LIFE LOOK LIKE WITHOUT SHAME?

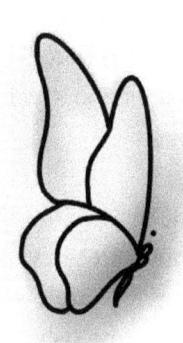

Alex (she/her) did not consciously question her sexuality until college. She went to the same school I did, Rhodes College, a stone building on a one-hundred-acre campus in Memphis, Tennessee, with its own quarry and the strangest mix of liberal and conservative students I'd ever seen. In so many ways, this was not the traditional college campus—our athletics got very little love, nearly everyone lived on campus all four years, and its small size and huge Greek-life population earned it the not-so-cute nickname of Lynx High. When only two thousand people go to a university, it feels like everyone knows everyone, and that pressure can be heavy. Despite this environment, Alex found a similar group of people like I did—folks genuinely interested in gender equity and in the study of sexuality and intercultural competencies. These patches of brilliant, accepting, engaged people were all over campus, and Alex found a place to flourish amongst them.

"Really, Rhodes was such a formative space for all of this. Just being in undergrad was such a different, freeing experience. I didn't really put it (her queerness) together until I was spending time with my now ex, Sarah." The two had been spending really meaningful time together, alone. Alex found herself using words like "interest" in her own mind to explain the way she was drawn to Sarah. "I was really interested in everything she had to say. I didn't even recognize that as attraction."

We don't all get this lucky when our brains don't let us register our true feelings, but Alex can vividly remember the day she realized her feelings for Sarah were more than platonic. After one of Memphis's notoriously rainy, muddy, wonderful arts festivals, she and Sarah escaped the storm into Sarah's apartment and spent hours together, just talking on the couch, tea in hand. "It kind of hit me all of a sudden. 'Oh, these are butterflies.'" Alex would get so excited to hang out with Sarah because she had a *crush* on her.

She didn't say anything to Sarah that afternoon but immediately went to Muddy's Cupcakes (the best cupcakes in the nation), and told one of her friends, Erin*, that she *liked a girl*.

I want to set the scene for you, dear reader, because this pastel-colored cupcake shop is about as whimsical as you can possibly imagine. The baristas learn your favorite cupcakes within weeks, and little gnome statues smile at you from nearly every corner of the cozy study spaces. Here is where Alex voiced her crush and let herself be vulnerable. I cannot think of a better place with Alex's regular order of a vanilla-vanilla Plane Jane on the plate before her.

During undergrad, Alex had been exposed to people who identified as LGBTQ+. This trusting environment allowed her the space and access to her own "aha" moment with the help of her favorite professor.

"Mark Behr, in his Queer Theory class around the same time I was spending time with Sarah and just beginning to put things together, asked, 'What would your life look like if you could do whatever felt pleasurable to you without any shame about it?'"

> # Well, what *would* your life look like if you could do whatever felt pleasurable to you without shame?
>
> MARK BEHR

Alex admitted to herself, "I was gravitating toward this person. If I could, I would be romantically involved with a woman."

Alex and Erin both come from conservative upbringings, but Alex's trust in her friend and her overwhelming giddiness from realizing her feelings pushed the words out. She couldn't contain herself, "I think the way I served it up to her was 'I think I'm in love with someone. And that someone is a girl.'" Alex did this as she was letting people into this part of her life a few more times after she and Sarah got together. She would begin the conversation with a statement about how happy she was, how positive all her feelings were, leaving little room for the listener to react poorly to the fact that her new partner was a woman. This little act of self-preservation helped her to feel confident that no one would argue with her. Because who would want to keep her from being happy? This is a clever idea that I will likely suggest to friends considering how to have this conversation in the future. Prioritizing happiness and joy to assure any skeptics in the validity and confidence in a queer relationship, I think, would be hard to push back on without looking like a jerk.

Alex had already been in queer, sex-positive, feminist spaces. As part of a lesbian-ish Margarita Night event, where you earned an invite for being "even the slightest bit queer," Alex would get teased for not being more vocally queer, more apt to choose a label for herself. "It could have also been internalized misogyny and discomfort around such a female-centric word." After some time in the relationship with Sarah, though, Alex found herself loving the word lesbian, its politics and its power.

"We started dating one night after hours and hours of conversation. Then around two in the morning, while she was walking me out to my car, she asked, 'Is this a friend thing or is this a more-than-a-friend thing?' That's exactly how she said it." Alex confirmed she was hoping for the latter, and they kissed. Sarah had dated women before and had been out as a lesbian since she was fifteen, and her confidence helped Alex name those feelings. But she still felt odd claiming lesbian, at least at first. The word has been sexualized for so long, and because this was the first woman Alex had dated, she did not know if she could claim that title.

"People at Rhodes used to call Sarah the straight girl whisperer. And she never seemed to have an outward problem with that. But once I had David Sedaris autograph a book for Sarah and he asked me the nature of our relationship." Sedaris, a famous gay humorist, asked if Sarah was Alex's girl friend or girlfriend, and when Alex stated they were together he wrote, 'To Sarah, a lesbian who likes to prey on younger women.' There was no context for this, and Sarah's reaction confirmed to Alex that the comment was pretty inappropriate. "And I gave it to her not knowing she had this hang up. Those kinds of comments were really hurtful for her. I think, because she presents as butch, she often had more femme women hit on her." The flirtations from overwhelmingly femme-presenting women was not an issue, but the assumption that Alex's femme presentation meant that some big-bad lesbian had "turned her" was gross and wrong. These are common jokes and Sedaris likely meant no real harm, but Alex had found a line that shouldn't be crossed.

Years later, the two are amicable toward one another but are no longer together. Alex lives in Atlanta and has been able to build a queer community for herself despite being in a new place. "I've been here for a little more than four years. I've dated around and I've been in some other more short-term relationships, but my partner now, Kyla, is nonbinary, and we've been dating for about a year. And so, I don't have the same attachment to the word lesbian anymore. Lesbian assumes you're dating another woman, and so I have weird feelings about using that now." Since dating Kyla, Alex has been drawn to "queer." "That's the word that feels most comfortable to me."

Alex is really good at checking in with her own comfort levels. She told me that at first, her understanding of queerness was very simple and very caught up in gender. "I think I have become much more aware of trans identities and concerns, and I feel generally more loving and not so stuck in so many boxes." She knows she's attracted to short haircuts and passionate personalities and does not feel the need to title those feelings differently anymore. Time and experience and openness to learning helped in her own identity confidence. "I won't say 'I only date these kinds of people.' Now, I'm able to talk about my desire in ways that don't cut people out because of the boxes they're put in. It's added a lot of nuance to my own understanding of desire, which feels very wonderfully humanizing and celebratory. Even dating apps, like Lex, are becoming inclusive of wider LGBTQ+ identities. With these small movements to accessible community-building, the better the community as a whole will become about connecting with one another.

Think of the unimagined potential you can realize in your own life. What would happen if you relaxed away from rigid thinking when it comes to sexuality and desire? Though not everyone feels sexual desire or romantic desire, for many people these things feel foundational to life. "Ask, 'what do I actually want and feel?' Come at it from more an emotion- and desire-based thinking. I wish I could tell little Alex, 'Yeah, there's a reason you keep looking at your cute camp counselor. She's beautiful.'"

SHAPE OF LOVE

When Valerie (she/her) was in college, she found a large, welcoming disability community.

"It was like this immediate home because the disability community is a really queer community, at least on the activism side." It seemed to Valerie like everybody she was around was both disabled and queer in some capacity. Finding herself attracted to groups of activists who identified with both communities, she was comfortable to present as entirely herself, in an unguarded fashion, to these new friends. Because an estimated three to five million LGBTQ+ people have disabilities, it didn't take too long for Valerie to find people with variations of each of these identifiers.[169]

"That's the first time I really remember feeling like I was safe. I was encompassed by acceptance in that space." Valerie mentioned that because there was a lot of bisexual-erasure when she was really figuring out who she was, it was difficult for her to really find home in the LGBTQ+ community. "I think finding that community (the disability community) changed everything for me because it made me be much more vocal with people, wanting to assert my queerness a little bit more."

Her relationship with the disability community is one connected through both chronic physical illness and mental illness. "It's an interesting place to be because I think there is still a bit of pushback from certain parts of the disability community, whether or not either (or both) of these less obvious disabilities 'count.'" She has both fibromyalgia and dysautonomia (POTs) as well as major depression and a personality disorder. Valerie thinks this debate largely has to do with the different mindsets on medicalizing symptoms. She struggled for almost a decade to get a doctor to listen to her, to get any type of diagnosis or treatment plan for her chronic illnesses.

Her experience with trying to get a mental illness diagnosis was hugely inconsistent, which, sadly, is far from an

---

169 "LGBT People with Disabilities," Arcus, August 21, 2019

uncommon story. She would receive a new diagnosis each time she saw a new psychiatrist, up until the last five years or so.

"I think it is getting better, but I am still hyper-aware of it anytime I am discussing disability in a room or on a panel. Because if I am not in a flare and using my cane, there's no indicator that I am disabled. And I worry how many disabled people in the audience think I am just another person speaking over them rather than from lived experience."

Despite these hesitancies, Valerie has found tremendous community, friendship, and support in the broader disability community from all different types of disabled people. When this welcoming feeling includes people who also identify as queer, Valerie feels at home.

She told me that within the LGBTQ+ and disability communities, however, some assumptions and biases still need to be challenged. "In high school, I was fat. The idea back then was that bisexuality didn't exist. You were either gay and hiding it, or desperate." Valerie was also presented in a feminine manner, so some people assumed she wasn't actually queer but just couldn't attract men either due to her weight or to her disability. "I wasn't fat and butch like my girlfriend. I wouldn't know until later how many queer disabled people also have their queerness associated with a desperate-ness." The discriminatory idea that folks with disabilities will take "whoever they can get" is awful on its own, and the ridiculous implication that this somehow makes this community more likely to need to be LGBTQ+ adds additional ignorance to the conversation. "They don't know that disabled people have sex and relationships and are straight and ace and pan and non-binary and all the things."

For many of Valerie's disabled friends, barriers to expressing their sexuality mostly stem from ableism, education, or lack of access in spaces and practice. Non-penetrative sex options both for queer and disabled people also do not get discussed nearly enough both within and outside of LGBTQ+ and disabled communities. Valerie's experience with Borderline Personality Disorder, though, was initially her biggest barrier. "If you know anything about it, Borderline Personality Disorder (BPD) has a 'bad' reputation. One weird 'symptom' of BPD is promiscuity. I have had many nights where I wonder if I live and love like I do because I have a disorder and not because it's what I like, but then I remember it doesn't matter." Even if Valerie's BPD contributes to her romantic and sexual preferences, "I would still be poly or queer because my 'disorder' is an integral part of me, not something to be cut out and hidden away. It's okay if it has affected how I love because I love my relationships. I adore my husband and my lovers and myself."

I wanted to chat with Valerie because she has been so vocal, despite concerns that her identities would not be believed. She was able to wait, to find herself in a space where she felt safe, to be loud about who she is and why people with similar experiences to hers need to be heard and represented.

Intersectional, make-space identity is apparent when talking to Valerie. Her pride in every community of which she is a part is apparent, but she did not always have the direct support to be so vocal. She found balance in reading poetry.

"By virtue of how I was raised I didn't really have any queer people in my life until I got much older, but I loved reading poets."

Valerie was a part of a spoken word poetry group when she was young, adventuring to poetry slams where a few key poets, she recalled with awe in her tone, performed. Hearing the boldness with which many of these poets spoke of their sexualities, Valerie found herself in the performance and art of it all. "The way they would talk about their lives, I think, taught me about queer love and queer heartbreak when I didn't have somebody to turn to." The first person Valerie ever loved was another woman while they were both in high school. Valerie went through her first queer relationship without being able to talk to her mother about the drama and excitement that comes with new love. When Valerie and her girlfriend got into fights and when they broke up, Valerie relied on poetry for both learning and for comfort.

The pattern in Valerie's story that I love is one of using a passionate voice to embolden others. Because Valerie was able to locate poets with the same priorities as she had, she found examples of how to later be emboldened to question the assumptions people even within the LGBTQ+ and disability communities have about one another. It can be uncomfortable to be in a family or community that is not welcoming, but people are often forming groups based on shared experiences, so they can usually be found if sought out.

Valerie's moment of clarity around self-acceptance and celebration came to her full force while she was at a sex party. There were many people with varying body types, genders, sexual orientations. She was fully naked in a living room, wearing her wedding ring, looking around at all these people. Some were chatting, some were having snacks, and some in various intimate activities. "I knew, with absolute certainty, I was comfortable there. I felt multiple levels of attraction and safety, but also felt seen and supported." It was a moment where all of Valerie's questions about vocabulary suddenly released from her focus. "I was Black enough. I was Hispanic enough. I was gay enough. What was me and what was my disorder, all of those questions stopped for a moment because I was in this… perfect image of my life in which I knew exactly who I was." Having that moment helped quiet those voices that made Valerie insecure about being "enough." While sex parties are not a necessity for lifting feelings of inadequacy, "There's nothing like standing naked in front of a bunch of people to make you really feel certain about who you are."

I asked Valerie what she would have liked a supportive adult to say to her when she was young and trying to navigate her sexuality and her surroundings. She thought for a moment, then said,

> "Love has so many more shapes than is represented in books and TV. We say 'there's no right way to love.' But we still really perpetuate it. We don't talk enough about the different ways you can be intimate and what that means. It's okay to want what you want."

SEEK OUT EXPERTS: IN KNOWLEDGE, SUPPORT, AND LOVING KINDNESS

In her book *Vice Versa: Bisexuality and the Eroticism of Everyday Life,* Dr. Marjorie Garber (she/her) introduces a brief history of bisexuality that I find particularly comforting in a world full of binaries and obsessions with solid, unmoving boundaries.[170] We often look at the world as a series of facts, and even once something is disproved, the

---

[170] Marjorie B. Garber, *Vice Versa: Bisexuality and the Eroticism of Everyday Life,* (New York: Simon and Schuster), 1995.

new fact is seen as unmovably true until proven otherwise. At least, this is my understanding of the way I've heard ideas discussed around me. It's either one truth or another, no in between. No gray areas. "The world is flat. The sun revolves around the earth. Human beings are either heterosexual or homosexual."[171]

We do this for good reason. Science is critical for society to function. We need to understand ourselves in order to create medicines, our surroundings to alleviate natural disasters, our neighbors to feel safe. Humanity relies on truths to function, even when the truths are biased or wrong. I find Dr. Garber's writings so appealing because she takes a no-nonsense approach to writing about bisexuality. Of course, the Earth isn't flat, and neither is human gender, sexuality, and romanticism.

"Alexander the Great had both male and female lovers. So did Julius Caesar. So, it turns out, did Sappho. And Socrates."[172] Historical evidence says bisexuality has been present for ages. It's not something cool a bunch of emo kids made up in 2008. I know this sounds like a no-brainer, but I can remember sitting up late at night in my early teen bedroom, punk rock posters on the green walls and magazines littering the bedside table, reading Tumblr posts about how girls who like girls only do it for attention and internalizing a fear that these disgusting posts were true. Don't get me wrong, I've had many an argument with many vocally straight women kissing other women at parties because it's

---

171 Garber, 1995.
172 Garber, 1995.

fun. Would I have those arguments again? No, particularly not the way I had them originally, but the point is that *my* sexuality isn't manifested that way. It's not a party trick for me, and that's important. But teenage me didn't know that and was terrified that I had some sort of weird kink I couldn't shake, not a valid sexuality.

I'm still figuring out how to make room for myself, which is difficult when even scientific studies are designed to exclude people "in the middle."

"What's interesting is that in order to come out with a judgment as to whether a gland or a gene is gay or straight, they have to throw out the middle category. They have to recode their bisexual subjects as either purely homosexual or purely heterosexual. So in fact the experiment produces the answer that it's designed to produce by creating what Hamer calls a dimorphic sample, an either or sample."[173]

Nothing in the middle exists. A multitude of potential sexual orientations to discover are wiped out in the styling of the study itself. Dr. Garber wrote about a piece in *Newsweek* where they were studying homosexual genes in fruit flies. Somewhere in the article, deeper than what is appropriate, the article talks about the fact that they classified any flies attracted to both female and male flies as homosexual.[174]

Yes, I understand these were fruit flies and not people. Yes, this may seem like a silly thing to worry about to people who

---

173 Garber, 1995.
174 Garber, 1995.

aren't constantly worried they are lying by omission. But I, dear readers, spend a good portion of my time fearing that I am a bad queer person because I don't make my identity obvious enough. And that's frustrating and stupid. If I'd married a woman, I think I would feel a similar dilemma, though the systemic pressures to appear straight would play a lesser role in the guilty feelings. I'd rather be an unsorted fruit fly, thank you very much. But the sorting happens over and over again.

So, what is there to do? I've mentioned in other chapters how difficult it is to study LGBTQ+ identities because the language around them is always changing. People can go through multiple labels themselves, and new terminology is invented and adopted every year. Self-identification is the core of the LGBTQ+ community. Queer people don't always have queer parents. The community must be sought out or built, depending on location and context. So, again, what exactly is there to do? In order for LGBTQ+ Revolution 2.0 to take hold, for the aspirations and hard work of those whose stories fill these pages to involve the multitudes of identities of our past and present, we must seek out experts. I don't just mean experts in academia but also those in support systems, community development, and those who are simply great examples of how to practice loving kindness.

Marjorie Garber is an expert, but so are Saeed Jones, Hafsa Qureshi, Kimberly Duron, and Kash. Alayna teaches courses on self-acceptance. Vishaal creates content that asserts our value. These celebratory narratives were honest and open in a way I think the movement requires. Not all these folks have PhDs, but they are experts in their own experiences, and this *matters*.

I'm sure plenty of LGBTQ+ researchers would tell you this, but I'm going to state it as plainly as I can. Write in your identity on any survey that isn't going to be linked specifically to your name (unless you aren't somebody who worries about privacy). Unless it's one of those horrible scantron situations from fill-in-the-bubble-sheet nightmares, you should be able to scribble some identifiers on the edges without it causing too much trouble. Online, see if you can find the people who created the survey and email them asserting the importance of having write-in opportunities in statistical research.

In groups, call out any sort of erasure or discriminatory jokes about particular identities by asking, "Can you explain that?" "Did someone say that Ben obviously only claims he is bisexual for attention because he married a woman?" Ask them if they'd talked to Ben about this. It's uncomfortable, I know. If you don't have the energy to do this all of the time, I understand. But taking actions like these can keep those you come into contact with aware that you listen when they talk and will respond to what they say, *especially* if it's exclusionary.

Seek out experts. Reading the works of people who spend their lives on this type of work in order to write this book has been profoundly healing. I've Googled things and fallen into identity traps online, but something about the current academic study of gender and sexuality is exciting and affirming. Reading experts helps me grasp that my intrigue and questions surrounding my own queerness is really not strange but expected. Loads of people have chosen to research the who and how and why around both LGBTQ+ identity and heteronormative behavior. Take Dr. Garber, for example. She is a Harvard professor who, in addition to Visual and Environmental Studies, has written books about *Cross-Dressing and Cultural Anxiety* and *Bisexuality and the Eroticism of Everyday Life*. How cool is that? Very! (I knew you knew the answer, but isn't it nice to be validated?) So read up, my friends, because it really does help in a pinch when you're trying to explain how pansexuality has nothing to do with kitchen utensils and that no, you don't want to sleep with everybody under the sun (unless you do, which, in case this hasn't been clear so far, is totally cool as long as it's consensual).

Scrolling for hours on Tumblr as a teenager, I'd been unknowingly seeking out experts on my identity and seeking some sense of validation. My methods for doing this same work now aren't perfect, but I'm learning how to distinguish the quality information from the misinformation.

Briefly, let's look back at the Greeks and Romans. In Garber's *Bisexuality and the Eroticism of Everyday Life*, she mentions that the Greek and Romans "lived so many years ago, and their culture had very different values. Besides, we say, they must have had a preference."[175]

They must have had a preference. I can specifically remember another post (I swear Tumblr wasn't solely toxic. There was a great amount of LGBTQ+ support on there. It's just that I

---

175 Marjorie B. Garber, *Vice Versa: Bisexuality and the Eroticism of Everyday Life*, (New York: Simon and Schuster), 1995.

would read threads in their entirety, even the unhelpful bits) where a number of bi, pan, and queer people were talking in-depth about their preferences. The difference between romantic and sexual attraction threw me through a huge, seemingly never-ending loop.

In the beginning of this project, I was focusing on my own experience as a bi, pan, and queer person. I knew going in that people who aren't straight and aren't 100 percent only attracted to their own gender can often be left out of both important academic studies and queer-affirming spaces, but I wasn't sure how that translated to the current LGBTQ+ movement and its challenges. I quickly discovered that Q+ included identities with which I was unfamiliar, and I am so glad I expanded what I thought this project would be because it led me to new ideas around queerness, representation, and community building.

In expanding my scope, I came across activists like Robyn and Valerie, examples of queer women using their experiences to change the superficial narratives and assumptions around bi and pansexuality, who we are, what we look like, and our greatest passions and concerns. Speaking with Vishaal and B completely reshaped the way I look at representation, on television and in movies and in daily life. Alexis and Hafsa pushed my understandings of how religion functions as it needs to for individuals and can provide shelter just as much as it does shame, depending on the person using it and its wider contexts. Cassandra, Alayna, and Kim assured me that my identity is my own and that communities can be sought out and built when needed, so long as one is willing to be vulnerable. Ari and River practiced this vulnerability online, building the necessary confidence to prioritize their own mental well-being. Xany and Kash walked me through their own coming out experiences in hopes that they might serve as evidence that while this vulnerability is never easy, the change it can have—the freedom and openness it provides—is worth the initial discomfort. Blair and Alex encouraged me to explore what I wanted out of this life and where the biases and elements of shame reside within me so I could learn to let them go.

Each of the individuals who provided narratives for this work or published ideas from which I drew inspiration made room for themselves in a way that aided my own LGBTQ+ identity formation. I am learning more and more how to ask for stories over opinions, experiences over assumptions, and openness over strict definitions.

Dear reader,

Seek out experts. Be safe. Make room. You are deserving of community and of peace. The voices that make up this collection do not assume to recognize you but hope to encourage you to share your own stories. Your joy is your resistance and there are those who hope to help you discover each little piece of yourself and how these multitudes layer beautifully together. The LGBTQ+ Revolution 2.0 isn't coming in the future or waiting on anyone in particular, but it is made out of us. We determine, now, how our generations will be seen—how and when we include one another. Your additions to the community, even simply accepting and celebrating yourself, makes this space, this movement. Who will you be, who and how will you love, without shame?

YOURS IN LEARNING,

JILL

ACKNOWLEDGMENTS

To Tony, my brilliant partner, master copy editor, and dog-dad, thank you for being the first reader of this book from draft to final edit, for talking me through crises and self-doubt, and for making me cheese-filled dinners. You're the absolute best.

To Tara and Mom, thank you for your thorough edits and unwavering support. I could not have finished this project without you both. Tara, your contributions helped me realize my knowledge gaps, even in this space.

Thank you to those of you who spent time speaking with me about your experiences as members of the LGBTQ+ community. Your vulnerability and willingness to chat, sitting in memories that weren't always comfortable, means the world to me and will matter so much to our readers. We have so much to celebrate.

Thank you to my Georgetown friends, especially Kim, Kash, Hélène, Hayley, Alejandro, and Ai-Hui, for allowing me to blab about how exciting an interview was or how worried I was during the writing process.

To my dear friends, Abbie and Madalyn, for taking the time to send me positive energy and feedback during the final edits.

To my Rhodes College family, I love you and miss you and cannot wait to see you all again.

Thank you to the New Degree Press team for giving me the tools necessary for the completion of this BOOK. A BOOK! Cass Lauer and Eric Koester, you were there from the beginning, helping me have the confidence to become an author. Brian Bies and Kim LaCoste, thank you for helping me put out fires and navigate promoting a book during COVID-19. This is such a weird moment for publishing. Thank you all for your work.

Lastly, thank you, reader, for your purchase. This book brings voices together in one compilation that I really could have used when I was young. You have made this resource, this party-in-pages, possible. We are all still learning. Thank you for your support.

This book would not have been possible without its earliest supporters:

Patricia Cisarik, Tony Hanna, Tara Fredenburg, Clark Fredenburg, Cody Lewis, Hans Davies, J.R. Osborn, Susan Sidamon-Eristoff, Neil Cronk, Peter Fredenburg, Daniel Dixon, Valerie Novack, Shannon Hoffman, Alexa DeJesus, Julie Chelius, Kate Colwell, Diana Owen, Treston Norphlet, Ai-Hui Tan, Daniel J Felleman, Andrew Bishop, Laurie Norris, Stephanie Kasper, Paul Hanna, Caitlin Bowers, Grace Hasson, Justin Davis, Andria Wisler, Allison Vas, Noelle Chaddock, Cynthia Ownby, Abbie Norris, Cass Lauer, Ted Harrison, Rhiannon Graybill, Yue Gong, Kimberly Duron, Kerin Maguire, Cynthia Anselmi, Sanjana Purker, Michael Clark, Michael Willson, Julia Dem, Kaitlyn Shamley, David Smalley, Xiebingqing Bai, Allison Sights, Madalyn Bryant, Michelle Ngo, Abbey Meller, Moruomi Li, Julia Proimina, Andreas Beissel, Hayley Pontia, Kim Pluskota, Pascal Girard, Kimberly Nicole Batson, Natalie Richmond, Jon Olav Eikenes, Catherine Miller, Xiaoman Chen, Elisabeth McDonald, Ashley Holden, Ian Turner, Tyler Adams, Alain Boussant, Julia Hamilton, Tate Mulligan, Nolu McIlraith, Yaolin Chen, Brynna E. Newkirk,Yutong Zhang, Joel P. Michelson, Alessandro Nigro, Zach Omer, Ozakh Ahmed, Allison Pickering, Sanjana Purker, Dezmone Valentine, Kaeya Humphries, Molly Mulhern, Hayden Longley, Victoria Dowdy, Aubrey Kearney, Karissa Coady, Dominik Booth, Josie Papazis, Leah Ford, and twelve anonymous readers.

RESOURCE LIST

You can find the sources of any specific quotes of interest in the citations within each chapter, but I thought I'd also gather a general list of resources for you.

For a wonderful and up-to-date expansion on LGBTQ+ vocabulary, please see Ash Mardell's book, *The ABC's of LGBT+*.[176] This book inspired my collection of narratives in many ways and goes into more detail about language and identifiers within queer community.

History.com has done great work compiling LGBTQ+ timelines in a "Gay Rights" section. Much of the information in the history acknowledgments at the beginning of this book was guided by the research found there.[177]

---

176 Ashley Mardell, *The ABC's of LGBT+*. (Mango Media Inc.), 2016.
177 History.com/topics/gay-rights/history-of-gay-rights.

The Human Rights Campaign has a handful of useful guides for anyone seeking information about coming out, seeking community, or general LGBTQ+ information.[178]

The Institute for Welcoming Resources lists religious organizations that are affirming to LGBTQ+ people.[179]

Lambda Literary advocates for LGBTQ writers, helping their stories reach the people who need them.[180]

The Trevor Project focuses on suicide prevention efforts among LGBTQ+ youth and is a great organization to follow on social media for affirmations and support.[181]

It Gets Better Project has identified over one thousand organizations in over forty countries that offer support to LGBTQ+ youth. Local resources are incredible spaces for connection for those who can locate them safely.[182]

GLAAD promotes LGBTQ+ acceptance through entertainment, news, and digital media.[183]

Safe Zone Project offers LGBTQ+ and ally trainings and workshops that I took part in during college. These trainings

---

178 "Advocating for LGBTQ Equality | Human Rights Campaign." Human Rights Campaign, April 26, 2020. hrc.org/.
179 Bischoff, Meredith. "The Institute for Welcoming Resources," accessed November 1, 2020. welcomingresources.org/.
180 LambdaLiterary.org
181 "The Trevor Project — Saving Young LGBTQ Lives." The Trevor Project, April 23, 2020. thetrevorproject.org/.
182 "Get Help." It Gets Better, April 11, 2019. itgetsbetter.org/get-help/.
183 Glaad.org

are helpful and sincere, creating a great opportunity for allies to learn how to better support their LGBTQ+ peers.[184]

StoryCorps has a "Stonewall Outloud" archive that is fun to sift through and also lists contributing organizations.[185]

There are so many fantastic LGBTQ+ organizations and resources on the web and in our neighborhoods. Reach out to these sources with questions, concerns, and community if you are having trouble finding the guidance or representation you deserve.

---

184 "Resources » The Safe Zone Project." The Safe Zone Project, May 2, 2020. thesafezoneproject.com/resources/.
185 "Stonewall OutLoud," May 3, 2020. storycorps.org/discover/outloud/.

APPENDIX

INTRODUCTION

Gates, Gary J. "How Many People are Lesbian, Gay, Bisexual, and Transgender?" *Williams Institute* (April, 2011). https://williamsinstitute.law.ucla.edu/publications/how-many people-lgbt/

Mardell, Ashley. *The ABC's of LGBT+*. Mango Media Inc., 2016.

AUTHOR'S NOTE

City Population. "Narva (Narva Linn, Ida-Viru, Estonia) - Population Statistics, Charts, Map, Location, Weather and Web Information". Accessed May 1, 2020. https://www.citypopulation.de/php/estonia-idaviru.php?cityid=0511.

Fundamental Rights Agency. "FRA - European Union Agency for Fundamental Rights," September 7, 2012. fra.europa.eu/fraWebsite/lgbt-rights/lgbt-rights_en.htm.

Liptak, Adam. "Supreme Court Ruling Makes Same-Sex Marriage a Right Nationwide," June 29, 2015. nytimes.com/2015/06/27/us/supreme-court-same-sex-marriage.html.

Mardell, Ashley. *The ABC's of LGBT+*. Mango Media Inc., 2016.

PBS. "Stonewall Inn: Through the Years | American Experience | PBS," accessed May 1, 2020. http://www.pbs.org/wgbh/americanexperience/features/stonewall-inn-through-years/.

A VERY BRIEF LGBTQ+ HISTORY: MOMENTS IN THE HISTORY OF THE GAY RIGHTS
Movement in the United States that Inform Our Paths Forward

Aizenman, Nurith. "How to Demand a Medical Breakthrough: Lessons from the AIDS Fight."

NPR.org, February 9, 2019. npr.org/sections/health-shots/2019/02/09/689924838/how-to-demand-a-medical-breakthrough-lessons-from-the-aids-fight.

Allen, Samantha. "Kinsey Was Wrong: Sexuality Isn't Fluid." The Daily Beast, April 13, 2017. https://www.thedailybeast.com/kinsey-was-wrong-sexuality-isnt-fluid

Bendix, Trish. "Queer Women History Forgot: Alice Dunbar-Nelson | GO Magazine," GO

Magazine, 22 March 2017. http://gomag.com/article/queer-women-history-forgot-alicedunbarnelson/

Brockell, Gillian. "The transgender women at Stonewall were pushed out of the gay rights movement. Now they are getting a statue in New York."The Washington Post. June 12, 2019. http://washingtonpost.com/history/2019/06/12/transgender-women-heart stonewall-riots-are-getting-statue-new-york/.

Bullough, Vern L. *Before Stonewall: Activists for Gay and Lesbian Rights in Historical Context.*

Routledge, 2002. https://doi.org/10.4324/9781315801681.

Center for Disease Control. "HIV and AIDS—United States, 1981—2000." June 1, 2001. cdc.gov/mmwr/preview/mmwrhtml/mm5021a2.htm.

Cheves, Alexander. "21 Words the Queer Community Has Reclaimed (and Some We Haven't)."

Advocate. Accessed June 4, 2020. advocate.com/arts entertainment/2017/8/02/21-words

queer-community-has-reclaimed-and-some-wehavent.

Cooper, Helene and Thomas Gibbons-Neff. "Trump Approves New Limits on Transgender

Troops in the Military." *New York Times.com*, accessed May 1, 2020. https://www.nytimes.com/2018/03/24/us/politics/trump-transgender-military.html

Domonoske, Camila. "'Kinder Gentler Indifference': Activists Challenge George H.W. Bush's Record On AIDS." NPR.org, December 4, 2018. npr.org/2018/12/04/673276127/kinder gentler-indifference-activists-challenge-george-h-w-bush-s-record-on-aids.

EIU Center for Gender and Diversity. "'Symbols within the GSD Community.'" Accessed February 1, 2020. eiu.edu/lgbtqa/symbolism.php.

Epstein, Reid, and Trip Gabriel. "Pete Buttigieg Drops Out of Democratic Presidential Race." March 2, 2020. nytimes.com/2020/03/01/us/politics/pete-buttigieg-drops-out.html.

Fox, Fallon. "Forget the Oscar: Jared Leto Was Miscast in Dallas Buyers Club." *Time*, March 4, 2014. time.com/12407/jared-leto-oscar-dallas-buyers-club-casting-trans-actors/.

Fort, Patrick. "Election of Transgender Lawmaker in Virginia Makes History." NPR.org, November 8, 2017. npr.org/2017/11/07/562679573/election-of-transgender-lawmaker-in-virginia-makes-history.

Healthline. "What's the Deal with the Kinsey Scale?" January 29, 2020. healthline.com/health/kinsey-scale#where-you-fall.

History.com. "Gay Rights." Jun 28, 2017 updated April 3, 2020. https://www.history.com/topics/gay-rights/history-of-gay-rights

Hitti, Natashah. "Daniel Quasar Redesigns LGBT Rainbow Flag to Be More Inclusive." Dezeen, June 19, 2019. dezeen.com/2018/06/12/daniel-quasar-lgbt-flag-inclusive/.

Human Rights Campaign. "Glossary of Terms | Human Rights Campaign." Accessed February 1, 2020. hrc.org/resources/glossary-of-terms.

Justia, "Military Service Members' Rights." accessed June 4, 2020. https://www.justia.com/lgbtq/militaryservice/.

Keehnen, Owen. "Radclyffe Hall | Legacy Project Chicago." Legacy Project Chicago. Accessed February 1, 2020. legacyprojectchicago.org/person/radclyffe-hall.

Krone, Mark. "Stonewall Was Important but Not Because It Was First." June 4, 2018. facingtoday.facinghistory.org/stonewall-was-important-but-not-because-it-was-first.

Morgan, Thad. "The Gay 'Sip-In' that Drew from the Civil Rights Movement to Fight Discrimination." History.com, Jun 18, 2018 updated April 12, 2019. https://www.history.com/news/gay-rights-sip-in-juslius-bar

National Park Service. "LGBTQ Activism: The Henry Gerber House, Chicago, IL (US National Park Service)." accessed February 1, 2020. nps.gov/articles/lgbtq-activism-henry--gerber-house-chicagoil.htm.

Out History. "Lesbians, World War II and Beyond (Cont) · Lesbians in the Twentieth Century, 1900-1999, OutHistory: It's About Time." Accessed May 1, 2020. outhistory.org/exhibits/show/lesbians-20thcentury/wwii-beyond/wwii-beyond-cont.

Levin, Sam. "Compton's Cafeteria Riot: A Historic Act of Trans Resistance, Three Years before Stonewall." The Guardian, June 21, 2019. theguardian.com/lifeandstyle/2019/jun/21/stonewall-san-francisco-riot-tenderloin-neighborhood-trans-women.

Mullen, Matt. "The Pink Triangle: From Nazi Label to Symbol of Gay Pride." History.com, July 9, 2019. https://www.history.com/news/pink-triangle-nazi-concentration-camps

Nagle, Rebecca. "The Healing History of Two-Spirit, A Term That Gives LGBTQ Natives A Voice." HuffPost, June 30, 2018. huffpost.com/entry/two-spirit identity_n_5b37cfbce-4b007aa2f809af1.

OnePULSE Foundation. "FAQs | OnePULSE Foundation." November 2, 2017. https://onepulsefoundation.org/faqs/

OUTMemphis. "About Us—OUTMemphis." April 26, 2020. https://www.outmemphis.org/about-us/

Peacock, Kent W. "Race, the Homosexual, and the Mattachine Society of Washington, 1961-1970." *Journal of the History of Sexuality* 25, no. 2 (2016): 267 296. https://www.muse.jhu.edu/article/614033.

"The AIDS Memorial Quilt: Learn More." Aids Memorial.org, November 20, 2019. aidsmemorial.org/theaidsquilt-learnmore/.

Plante, Hank. "Reagan's Legacy." *San Francisco AIDS Foundation*, February 10, 2011, sfaf.org/collections/status/reagans-legacy/
Qureshi, Hafsa. "Too Queer to Be Muslim,

Too Muslim to Be Queer." News.trust.org, Feb. 25, 2019. news.trust.org/item/20190225100111-i2g1a/.

"Same-Sex Couples Can Now Adopt Children In All 50 States." Accessed June 4, 2020.

Governing.com. https://www.governing.com/topics/health-human-services/Same-Sex

Couples-Can-NowAdopt-Children-in-All-50-States.html.

Stults, Christopher. "Perceptions of Safety Among LGBTQ People Following the 2016 Pulse

Nightclub Shooting." *PubMed Central (PMC)*, September 2017. ncbi.nlm.nih.gov/pmc/articles/PMC5693229/.

Tran, Chrysanthemum. "When Remembering Stonewall, We Need to Listen to Those Who

Were There." *Them.*, June 11, 2020. them.us/story/who-threw-the-first-brick-at-stonewall.

US Food and Drug Administration, "Coronavirus (COVID-19) Update: FDA Provides Updated

Guidance to Address the Urgent Need for Blood During the Pandemic." 2 Apr. 2020. fda.gov/news-events/press-announcements/coronavirus-covid-19-update-fda-provides updated-guidance-address-urgent-need-blood-during-pandemic.

MISTY: CALLED ME OUT

Movement Advancement Project, BiNet USA, and Bisexual Resource Center. "Understanding Issues Facing Bisexual Americans." 2014. https://www.lgbtmap.org/understanding-issues-facing-bisexual-americans

Gedlinske, Misty. "Bisexuality: The Invisible Letter 'B' | Misty Gedlinske | TEDxOshkosh." YouTube, 22 January 2019, youtube.com/watch.

VISHAAL: OPPORTUNITY AND MEDIA REPRESENTATION

Beatriz, Stephanie. "Stephanie Beatriz Is Bi and Proud as Hell." *GQ*, 21 June 2020, gq.com/story/stephanie-beatriz-is-bi-and-proud-as-hell.

Bohemian Rhapsody. Twentieth Century Fox Home Entertainment, 2019.

Dallas Buyers Club. Focus Features, 2013.

Fallon Fox. "Forget the Oscar: Jared Leto Was Miscast in Dallas Buyers Club." *Time*, March 4, 2014. https://time.com/12407/jared-leto-oscar-dallas-buyers-club-casting-trans-actors/

Jackman, Josh. "Demi Lovato Has Revealed the Truth about Her Sexuality." PinkNews, June 26, 2019. pinknews.co.uk/2018/03/07/demi-lovato-has-opened-up-about-her-sexuality/.

Lamont, Tom. "Harry Styles: 'I'm Not Just Sprinkling in Sexual Ambiguity to Be Interesting.'" The Guardian, December 15, 2019. theguardian.com/music/2019/dec/14/harry-styles-sexual-ambiguity-dating-normals-rocking-a-dress.

Levine, Nick. "Who Was the Real Freddie Mercury?" BBC. October 11, 2019. bbc.com/culture/story/20191010-who-was-the-real-freddie-mercury.

Nichols, James. "Felicity Huffman Discusses Cisgender Actors Playing Transgender Roles."

HuffPost, February 2, 2016. huffpost.com/entry/felicity-huffman-transgender-actors_n_5902314.

Spanos, Brittany. "Janelle Monáe Frees Herself." Rolling Stone, June 25, 2018. rollingstone.com/music/music-features/janelle-monae-frees-herself-629204/.

Transamerica. Belladonna Productions, 2005.

Transparent 1-5. Amazon Prime, 2015.

UCLA College of Social Sciences. "Hollywood Diversity Report 2019: Old Story, New

Beginning." 2019. https://socialsciences.ucla.edu/wp-content/uploads/2019/02/UCLA Hollywood-Diversity-Report-2019-2-21-2019.pdf

ROBYN: VULNERABILITY TO ACTIVISM

CCGSD. "The Gender Elephant." July 25, 2018. ccgsd-ccdgs.org/gender-elephant/.

Merriam-Webster.com. s.v. "Singular 'They.'" Accessed February 1, 2020. https://www.merriam-webster.com/words-at play/singular-nonbinary-they.

"To All the People Wondering Whether Bi Is Trans Exclusionary: LEARN OUR HISTORY, FFS: Bisexual." 2020. Reddit.com, accessed February 1, 2020. https://www.reddit.com/r/bisexual/comments/eo2vah/to_all_the_people_wondering_wh her_bi_is_trans/.

Zane, Zachary. "What's the Real Difference between Bi- and Pansexual?" Rolling Stone, October 4, 2019. rollingstone.com/culture/culture-features/whats-the-real-difference-between-bi-and-pansexual-667087/.

STACY: Q AND *OC*

Human Rights Campaign. "Being African American & LGBTQ: An Introduction | Human

Rights Campaign," accessed February 1, 2020. hrc.org/resources/being-african-american-Lgbtq-an-introduction.

LGBTQ Funders. "People of Color—Funders for LGBT Issues," accessed February 1, 2020. lgbtfunders.org/resources/issues/people-of-color/.

RIVER: ASEXUAL IDENTITY

Lacy, Adriana. "The Hypersexualization of the LGBTQ Community Is Still a Significant Issue

The Underground." The Underground, September 1, 2016. psuunderground.com/2016/09/01/the-hypersexualization-of-the-lgbtq-community-is-still-a-significant-issue/.

LGBTQ Life at Williams. "10 Things You Need to Know about Asexuality." May 1, 2020. lgbt.williams.edu/homepage/10-things-you-need-to-know-about-asexuality/.

XANY: COMING OUT IS ALMOST ALWAYS SCARY

Lees, Mark. "Coming Out as a Bisexual Man: The 5 Reasons Why We Don't—Bisexual

Resource Center." November 6, 2019. biresource.org/coming-out-as-a-bisexual-man-the-5-reasons-why-wedont/.

Mardell, Ashley. *The ABC's of LGBT+*. Mango Media Inc., 2016.

Pew Research Center. "Chapter 3: The Coming Out Experience." Pew Research Center's Social & Demographic Trends Project, December 31, 2019. pewsocialtrends.org/2013/06/13/chapter-3-the-coming-out-experience/.

ARI: ONLINE COMMUNITY

Burns, Katelyn. "The Internet Made Trans People Visible. It Also Left Them More Vulnerable." Vox, December 27, 2019. vox.com/identities/2019/12/27/21028342/trans-visibility backlash-internet-2010.

Greenberg, Daniel. "America's Growing Support for Transgender Rights | PRRI." PRRI, accessed May 1, 2020. prri.org/research/americas-growing-support-for-transgender-rights/.

Mardell, Ashley. *The ABC's of LGBT+*. Mango Media Inc., 2016.

Song, Sandra. "Kat Blaque Doesn't Give a Fuck." PAPER, September 11, 2019. papermag.com/kat-blaque-youtube-2639319887.html.

TRISHA: IT CAN BE SMALL

Margolies, Lynn, and PhD Margolies. "Competition among Women: Myth and Reality." Psych Central, October 8, 2018. psychcentral.com/lib/competition-among-women-myth-and reality/.

VALERIE: FINDING VOCABULARY

EurekAlert! "Many LGBTQ Youth Don't Identify with Traditional Sexual Identity Labels." February 13, 2019. eurekalert.org/pub_releases/2019-02/uoc-mly021319.php.

"Family Services of Peel." Family Services of Peel, April 12, 2019. fspeel.org/services/counselling/lgbttqqiaap/.

Wang, Hansi. "2020 Census Will Ask about Same-Sex Relationships." NPR.org, March 30, 2018. npr.org/2018/03/30/598192154/2020-census-will-ask-about-same-sex relationships.

HAFSA: IDENTITY IN MULTITUDES

Bischoff, Meredith. "The Institute for Welcoming Resources." Accessed March 2020. welcomingresources.org/.

Fishberger, Jeffrey, Phoenix Schneider, and Henry Ng. "Coming Out as You." The Trevor Project, January 2017. https://www.thetrevorproject.org/wpcontent/uploads/2017/09/Coming-OutAsYou.pdf

Qureshi, Hafsa. "Too Queer to Be Muslim, Too Muslim to Be Queer." news.trust.org, February 25, 2019. https://news.trust.org/item/20190225100111-i2g1a/

The Odyssey Online. "Feminist Muslim Warrior Series: Khawla Bint Al Azwar, The Muslim Mulan." October 17, 2019. theodysseyonline.com/feminist-muslim-warrior-series-khawla bint-al-azwar-the-muslim-mulan.

FANFIC AS DISCOVERY

Jenkins, Henry. "'Welcome to Bisexuality, Captain Kirk': Slash and the Fan-Writing-Community." In Textual Poachers: Television Fans and Participatory Culture, 237–74. Routledge, 2013. https://doi.org/10.4324/9780203114339-12.

ʻOkun, Alanna. "Why Are So Many Gay Romance Novels Written by Straight Women? Electric Literature." Electric Literature, March 21, 2019. electricliterature.com/why-are so-many-gay-romance-novels-written-by-straight-women/.

Randel, Jane, and Amy Sánchez. "Parenting in the Digital Age of Pornography." HuffPost, February 26, 2017. huffpost.com/entry/parenting-in-the-digital-age-of pornography_b_9301802.

Townsend, Megan, Director Research, and Analysis Research. "GLAAD's 'Where We Are on TV' Report Shows TV Is Telling More LGBTQ Stories than Ever." GLAAD, November 7, 2019. glaad.org/blog/glaads-where-we-are-tv-report-shows-tv-telling-more-lgbtq stories-ever.

CASSANDRA: FINDING COMMUNITY IN SUBTLETY

Catalyst. "Lesbian, Gay, Bisexual, and Transgender Workplace Issues: Quick Take | Catalyst." June 17, 2019. catalyst.org/research/lesbian-gay-bisexual-and-transgender-workplaceissues/.

Wang, Hansi. "2020 Census Will Ask About Same-Sex Relationships." NPR.org, March 30, 2018. npr.org/2018/03/30/598192154/2020-census-will-ask-about-same-sex relationships.

KASH: COMING OUT TWICE

Them. "Butch Women Talk About What It Means to Be Butch." YouTube, 2017.

Wang, Hansi. "2020 Census Will Ask about Same-Sex Relationships." NPR.org, March 30, 2018. npr.org/2018/03/30/598192154/2020-census-will-ask-about-same-sex relationships.

HAFSA: IDENTITY IN MULTITUDES

Bischoff, Meredith. "The Institute for Welcoming Resources." Accessed March 2020. welcomingresources.org/.

Fishberger, Jeffrey, Phoenix Schneider, and Henry Ng. "Coming Out as You." The Trevor Project, January 2017. https://www.thetrevorproject.org/wpcontent/uploads/2017/09/Coming-OutAsYou.pdf

Qureshi, Hafsa. "Too Queer to Be Muslim, Too Muslim to Be Queer." news.trust.org, February 25, 2019. https://news.trust.org/item/20190225100111-i2g1a/

The Odyssey Online. "Feminist Muslim Warrior Series: Khawla Bint Al Azwar, The Muslim Mulan." October 17, 2019. theodysseyonline.com/feminist-muslim-warrior-series-khawla bint-al-azwar-the-muslim-mulan.

FANFIC AS DISCOVERY

Jenkins, Henry. "'Welcome to Bisexuality, Captain Kirk': Slash and the Fan-Writing-Community." In Textual Poachers: Television Fans and Participatory Culture, 237–74. Routledge, 2013. https://doi.org/10.4324/9780203114339-12.

'Okun, Alanna. "Why Are So Many Gay Romance Novels Written by Straight Women? Electric Literature." Electric Literature, March 21, 2019. electricliterature.com/why-are so-many-gay-romance-novels-written-by-straight-women/.

Randel, Jane, and Amy Sánchez. "Parenting in the Digital Age of Pornography." HuffPost, February 26, 2017. huffpost.com/entry/parenting-in-the-digital-age-of pornography_b_9301802.

Townsend, Megan, Director Research, and Analysis Research. "GLAAD's 'Where We Are on TV' Report Shows TV Is Telling More LGBTQ Stories than Ever." GLAAD, November 7, 2019. glaad.org/blog/glaads-where-we-are-tv-report-shows-tv-telling-more-lgbtq stories-ever.

CASSANDRA: FINDING COMMUNITY IN SUBTLETY

Catalyst. "Lesbian, Gay, Bisexual, and Transgender Workplace Issues: Quick Take | Catalyst." June 17, 2019. catalyst.org/research/lesbian-gay-bisexual-and-transgender-workplaceissues/.

Wang, Hansi. "2020 Census Will Ask About Same-Sex Relationships." NPR.org, March 30, 2018. npr.org/2018/03/30/598192154/2020-census-will-ask-about-same-sex relationships.

KASH: COMING OUT TWICE

Them. "Butch Women Talk About What It Means to Be Butch." YouTube, 2017.

ALAYNA: WHY STIR THE POT?

"Draw My Life (Coming Out)" Alayna Joy, YouTube, 2015. https://www.youtube.com/watch?v=Cr9Dd_sHC7I

Mardell, Ashley. *The ABC's of LGBT+*. Mango Media Inc., 2016.

"The wedding is off. | Coming Out Again" Alayna Joy, YouTube, 2020. https://www.youtube.com/watch?v=Nl_Ja4_7Rfo

KIM: YOUR IDENTITY IS YOURS

Joel, Samantha. "3 Myths About Bisexuality, Debunked by Science." Psychology Today, May 22, 2014. psychologytoday.com/us/blog/dating-decisions/201405/3-myths-about bisexuality-debunked-science.

Scott, Izabella. "How the Cyberfeminists Worked to Liberate Women through the Internet." Artsy, October 13, 2016. https://www.artsy.net/article/artsy-editorial-how-the-cyberfeminists-worked-to- liberate-women-through-the-internet

Thorpe, J.R. "Why Won't Some People Date Bisexuals?" Bustle, September 8, 2016. bustle.com/articles/182670-why-wont-some-people-date-bisexuals-a-new-study confirms-that-biphobia-is-still-alive.

BLAIR: EXPLORATION

Hida. "How Common Is Intersex? An Explanation of the Stats—Intersex Campaign for Equality." Intersex Equality, April 1, 2015. intersexequality.com/how-common-is-intersex-in- humans/#:~:text=How%20Common%20is,An%20

Explanation%20of%20the%20Stats.&-ext=The%20most%20 thorough%20existing%20research,hair%20(1%25%2D2%25).

SHAPE OF LOVE

Arcus. "LGBT People with Disabilities—Arcus." August 21, 2019. arcusfoundation.org/publications/lgbt-people-with-disabilities.

SEEK OUT EXPERTS: IN KNOWLEDGE, SUPPORT, AND LOVING KINDNESS

Garber, Marjorie. *Vice Versa: Bisexuality and the Eroticism of Everyday Life*. (New York: Simon and Schuster, 1995.) prelectur.stanford.edu/lecturers/garber/viceversa.html.

CPSIA information can be obtained
at www.ICGtesting.com
Printed in the USA
LVHW021703031120
670607LV00014B/1977